UFOs
at the
Drive-in

100 True Cases of Close Encounters at Drive-In Theaters

Preston Dennett

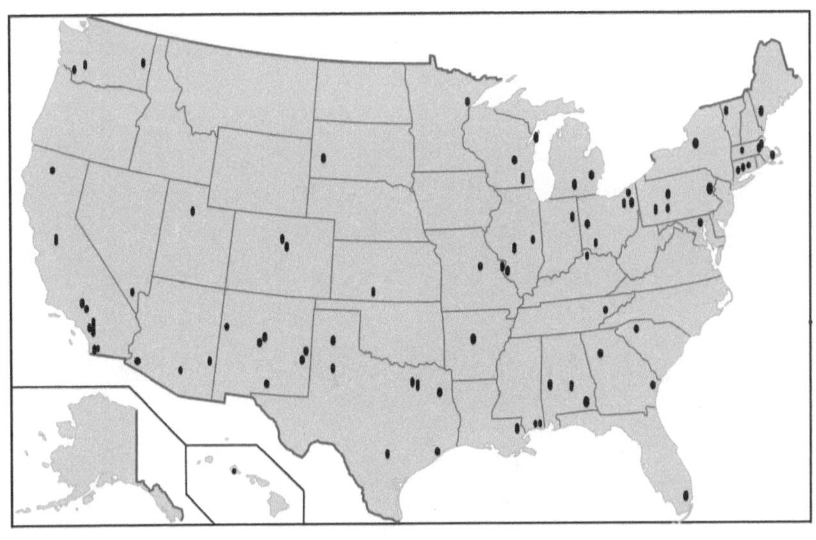

UFOs at the Drive-In: 100 True Cases of Close Encounters at Drive-In Theaters.

Blue Giant Books

Non-Fiction

ISBN: 9798657067569

1.   UFOs, Extraterrestrials, Aliens. 2. New Age, Metaphysical, Occult, Paranormal, Supernatural. 3. Movies, Entertainment. 4. Science, Astronomy. I. Title

Cover Art by Christine Kesara Dennett. Website: www.kesara.org/

CONTENTS

Introduction

"I can cite the exact time I first became interested in UFOs...My mother, my older brother and I were at a drive-in theater...I looked out the righthand side of the car and saw one of the most dramatic, bizarre-looking things I've ever seen in my life...The reason I'm the director of the National UFO Reporting Center today is because of that sighting."

--Mark Davenport, Director of NUFORC

I had investigated UFOs for many years when I first met a young woman by the name of Claudia Blacios. She was a new co-worker at my place of employment. When she found out that I was a UFO researcher, she proceeded to tell me an incredible story. Back in 1972, when she was a young child, her parents took her to a drive-in movie theater in Paramount, California. At some point during the movie, a UFO showed up -- a silver, metallic disc, hovering right next to the movie screen. The crowd of movie-goers panicked and chaos ensued.

It was an amazing encounter. I marveled at the audacity of the UFO occupants to brazenly swoop down and show themselves fearlessly to a large crowd of people. I had never heard of anyone seeing UFOs at a drive-in theater before, certainly not like this.

It wasn't until several years later, when I wrote *UFOs over California* that I ran into a few other cases. Still, I didn't think much of it. I continued to write books about other states, and found more cases. But it wasn't until I was doing research for *UFOs over Colorado* that I ran into three cases in a row. That's when I realized that there was something very strange happening here. UFOs were targeting drive-in movie theaters.

Intrigued, I decided to dig a little deeper. Little did I realize what I was getting into. I thought researching this subject might be a fun, breezy little investigation into a curious and unique type of UFO encounter. I was sure there were other cases out there, but I certainly didn't think they were very common.

To my amazement, I found a huge number of cases. Most of them were not well-known, and yet they were usually very striking low-level encounters. In case after case, the UFOs put on a show that was often far better than the movie itself. In many cases there were bizarre electromagnetic effects. Several of the cases were so dramatic that it caused panic, with people dropping everything and fleeing the theater in terror. In one case, there were human casualties as a result of the panic. There were cases in which police or government officials become involved. Some cases pushed the boundary even further, involving humanoids, missing time, and even one case involving an apparent observed abduction.

It was instantly obvious that there was something unique and special about these types of cases. These were not simple random sightings. When it comes to UFOs visiting drive-in theaters, it appears that the ETs are fully aware that they are being observed, and are intentionally showing themselves. There is good reason to believe, I think, that they are using drive-in movies as an opportunity to announce their presence and show themselves off to groups of people.

As I began collecting and documenting the many cases, I realized that I had stumbled upon an area of UFO activity that had been occurring for at least seventy years, but had somehow been largely ignored, even by the UFO community. This was amazing because the cases themselves were so spectacular.

UFOs behave in ways that, at first look, might appear to be random and unpredictable. An analysis of the massive data base of encounters, however, reveals some truly startling patterns. UFO sightings may seem random, but many of them are not. UFOs often appear for very specific reasons and are drawn toward particular areas or activities. Investigators call these "UFO attractors." I have already studied and written about several of these. Some examples include graveyards, rocket launches, prisons and mines. My book, *Schoolyard UFO Encounters*, focuses solely on one type of UFO attractor: schools.

Each of these areas have highly-specialized uses for human beings. Each represent a very important human activity that could be considered vital for a growing, well-functioning society. For whatever reason, UFOs are attracted to them.

And as this book will show, another UFO attractor that has received almost no attention are drive-in movie theaters. In case after case, drive-in theaters have been targeted by UFOs. And not at day, but while the movie is actually playing.

What is it about drive-ins that UFOs find so attractive? Could it be that the gigantic movie screens flashing provocative images are catching their eye? Are they there for entertainment, just like us? Are they studying our movies to learn about us? Could it be, as a few people mentioned to me, that the ETs see the audience members as "easy pickings?" What exactly is going on here? Furthermore, what exactly happens when a UFO suddenly appears unannounced in front of a large crowd of people?

Cases like these are both fascinating and numerous. One early drive-in UFO encounter occurred to David Roybal, a journalist from Santa Fe, New Mexico. He is among the first to speculate on the possibility that drive-ins attract UFOs.

It was the mid-1950s. The Modern Age of UFOs had just begun. "I've got to confess to having a special interest," Roybal writes. "As a kid of thirteen, I spotted lights racing, circling, bobbing, disappearing and reappearing in the night sky between Santa Fe and Los Alamos. I never had seen anything like it. Nor have I seen anything like it since. Until I hear a logical explanation for it, I can't discount the possibility that we've been visited by something extraterrestrial."

Where did he see them? "They'd need something to do once they arrived," Roybal says. "Surely the aircraft I spotted years ago near Santa Fe's southside weren't hovering over the Yucca Drive-In to get a free look at Frankie Avalon and Annette Funicello on the big screen."

Or were they? At that time, UFOs hovering over drive-ins was still a new phenomenon. Roybal admits that he still has no idea what he saw, and he is okay with that. As he says, "A newspaperman's life, I guess, wouldn't be much fun without mysteries."

Why are UFOs attracted to drive-in theaters? This is, of course, the million-dollar question.

Drive-ins have certainly held a strong fascination for humans. In their heyday of the 1950s, they were extremely popular family attractions. Theater owners used a wide variety of gimmicks to attract customers. Beyond the snack bars and concession stands, there were balloon rides, petting zoos, prize giveaways, and live pre-shows of all kinds. Many had a fully-equipped playground for kids to play. Some had bleachers. All of these "extras" served to make drive-in movies one of the most popular American past-times.

By the 1960s, the drive-in theater's popularity was still strong, but its reputation began to change. They had always been popular among dating couples, but sometimes the physical relations in various cars became a bit too intimate. The media began to label drive-ins as "passion pits." Some theaters hired policemen to walk up and down the rows of cars with a flashlight in hand, warning couples to keep their heads above the seat. Drive-in theaters, it seems, are fertile places for all kinds of human experiences.

While people were watching outdoor movies in their cars as early as 1915, the world's first public drive-in theater opened in June 1933. It never made a profit and three years later, after changing several owners, it closed down. The second oldest is Shankweiler's Drive-In in Orefield, Pennsylvania. It was opened in 1934 and is the oldest drive-in theater still operating today.

The most popular drive-in theater name is "Starlite." Not surprisingly, three theaters with this name appear in this book. Currently New York, with about twenty-eight operating theaters, has the most of any state. The largest known drive-in, the Ford Wyoming Drive-in Theater in Dearborn, Michigan can hold up to 3000 cars. But the Swap-Shop Drive-in Theater in Fort Lauderdale, Florida has fourteen screens, more than any other theater.

Today there are approximately 325 drive-in theaters still operating in the United States. Compare that to the 1950s and 1960s when there were at least 4000 operating theaters, and it becomes clear that the golden age of drive-in theaters is now over.

In the 1980s, there was a steep drop in the number of theaters. Many reasons are believed to have caused the decline:

the advent of daylight savings time which pushed back the starting time for movies significantly later, and the invention of VHS and CDs, which allowed home movie viewing. Also, advances in technology made it difficult for drive-in movie theaters to transition. Despite making a recent modest come-back, it will probably never be like it used to be.

But this hasn't stopped the UFOs from appearing over drive-ins to show themselves off. Cases reach back to 1950 and are still continuing today.

The accounts in this book come from a wide variety of sources, including newspaper articles, the massive databases of various UFO organizations such as MUFON, NUFORC, APRO, CUFOS and NICAP, books and articles, the USAF's Blue Book archives, and of course from firsthand interviews with the witnesses.

A few researchers have provided cases. Peter Davenport, head of NUFORC, is one example. Many other investigators have come across cases like these including (but not limited to) Scott Colborn, Lawrence Fawcett, Loren Gross, Ryan Sprague, John Timmerman, Brian Vike, and Linda Zimmerman.

Because nobody's ever really looked at drive-in movie UFO encounters before, I'm confident that most people (even those knowledgeable about UFOs) will find these cases brand new. Only a very few of them have ever appeared in book form and some cases are published here for the first time.

This is a small book, but it is also unique and, I think, ground-breaking. It is the first (and only) comprehensive collection and exploration of UFO drive-in theater encounters, and it reveals some intriguing insights into the extraterrestrial agenda. More than 100 cases are presented, each involving an incident in which UFOs visited a drive-in theater. The cases are presented chronologically, as they happened.

Each case is different. They are alternately puzzling, amusing, thrilling, awe-inspiring, concerning, and even terrifying. Each case provides a startling glimpse into a very strange type of UFO behavior that is only rarely seen.

UFOs at the Drive-In will take you on an exciting and surprising journey that is sure to change the way you feel about UFOs.

Starlite Drive-In Theater

The earliest drive-in UFO encounter on record ended up reaching very high levels of military intelligence, perhaps because by lucky coincidence, the main witness, Vernon Gwynne, was a newspaper journalist.

On July 22, 1950, Gwynne and his wife Betty visited the Starlite Drive-In Theater in Spartanburg, South Carolina. The lot was crowded with other cars. At some point midway through the movie, Gwynne noticed a "flying something" overhead. It was to be the first of three appearances.

"I first noticed a cloud-like formation that was driving in the opposite direction of the other clouds," Gwynne says. "This cloud was very low and indistinct. I called Betty's attention to it and asked her if she noticed anything peculiar about it. As we watched, it took a more definite shape which was rounded on the bottom and fairly flat.

"Since we wanted others to be able to corroborate our story, I got out of the car and asked two fellows in the next car, 'Look up there and see if you see what we see?' By the time they looked, the something was gone.

"The second time, I saw the cloud forming in the same place, apparently out of the clear sky. The fellows in the car, Betty and I watched the shape form in the center of the 'cloud.' After about two or three minutes, the shape disappeared again.

"About thirty minutes later," Gwynne continues, "all four of us again saw the shape, only this time it was very clearly lighted and had changed position...The color of the rounded bottom was about the same as a reflected fire on a silver or white surface. The size we would estimate to be larger than any dirigible we have ever seen...We discussed it and asked each other how we are going to describe it. We are convinced that we saw what other people say are 'Flying Saucers.'"

The object appeared to be about 2000 feet high, though somewhat lower on its third appearance. Gwynne submitted a report to the Air Force.

The case was routed to Project Blue Book, and a long report was written up. The report, titled "Flying Thing," described the encounter in-depth, and said, "Mr. Gwynne stated that he did not know what the object was, but that he had never seen anything like it before, and that he, his wife, and the other two observers all agreed that its structural appearance, its behavior in the air, and its tremendous size eliminated it being any aircraft known by the four of them."

The entire report, titled "Unconventional Aircraft," was forwarded to Colonel John Meade, Commanding General, Air Material Command, at Wright-Patterson Air Force Base in Dayton, Ohio. Clearly, the U.S. military was taking reports of UFOs very seriously.

Fair Park Drive-In Theater

The earliest drive-in encounters are relatively tame. While it does appear that the UFOs are showing themselves intentionally, it's typically only for a short while, almost as if they are "testing the waters," before diving into the deep end.

The second encounter on record, although, brief, has the earmark "showing off" behavior that is seen so often in drive-in UFO cases.

On the evening of September 25, 1950, deputy sheriff Aubrey Yates of Jefferson County, Alabama, and his wife decided to attend a movie at the Fair Park Drive-In. They were about half-way through the movie when Yates and his wife saw a "cigar-shaped object right above the screen."

Yates was amazed. "My wife saw it too, and we watched it for about fifteen minutes," the deputy said. "It looked like a cigar burning on both ends -- two big glows with a kind of soft glow in-between. Then all at once, the thing disappeared. It went straight up and disappeared in about three seconds."

Yates reported his sighting to the *Birmingham Post-Herald*. As it turned out, the U.S. Weather Bureau at the local airport received "several" calls describing the same type of object.

These first encounters opened the floodgates. From this point on, UFO drive-in encounters would occur with incredible regularity. In fact, the next case occurred almost exactly one month later.

Oak Ridge Drive-In Theater

This next account, from U.S. Army Intelligence records, provides the third case of a drive-in movie UFO encounter. The incident began precisely at 6:23 p.m., October 24, 1950, when radar operators at the Knoxville Airport in Knoxville, Tennessee detected several small slow-moving targets in a "restricted flying zone" over Oak Ridge, Tennessee. The radar operators tracked the objects for three minutes as they moved from the city area to the eastern boundary. A jet fighter was scrambled and vectored to the target. The pilot, however, was unable to obtain any visual confirmation of the objects.

Meanwhile, about fifteen minutes later, at 6:45 p.m., audience members at a nearby drive-in were enjoying a presentation of the latest film, when one of the UFOs showed up. By coincidence, one of the audience members was William B. Fry, the Assistant Chief of Security at the NEPA Division of Oak Ridge. Fry was there with his wife and child. All three saw "an object" glowing and changing in color from red, green, blue and orange. The unknown object moved back and forth at about thirty degrees height in a horizontal trajectory.

The projectionist was alerted to the presence of the UFO and admitted that he could see it. Another witness who lived nearby, Air Force Major Lawrence Ballweg, observed the object from his residence. At 7:20 p.m., after a long display lasting thirty-seven minutes, the object finally disappeared.

Fairview Drive-In Theater

It was a Sunday evening on July 8, 1951 and officer Robinson of the 3814 Installation Squadron at Maxwell Air Force Base, Alabama had a rare night off. He decided to drive off-base to the nearby Fairview Drive-In Theater and catch a movie.

Around 8:35 p.m., Robinson was watching the movie when he noticed a glowing disc-shaped "thing" in the sky. Following the experience, Robinson was interrogated by Air Force Officers about the sighting. The official report on Robinson's sighting says:

"The object observed by Robinson appeared to be saucer-shaped, very thin at the outer edges and comparatively thick toward the center section. Robinson said that the object glowed with a light that was comparable to the bluish light given off by desk lights. Robinson further states that the object appeared to be about two and one-half miles southeast of the Fairview Drive-In Theater...and that the object appeared to be at an elevation of approximately 1000 feet."

Robinson estimated that the object was about fifty to seventy-five feet in diameter. He watched it for about six seconds as it floated and wobbled, when it suddenly accelerated extremely quickly toward the south.

Robinson was interviewed by Lt. Colonel Hays of the Air Force OSI, who wrote, "During the interview, Robinson gave the impression that he is a mature, level-headed and intelligent type of person."

For a drive-in encounter, it's a brief sighting. But at this point, the wave of drive-in encounters had only just begun. Again, the early encounters are relatively simple. The 1950s is more like the pre-show. The real action would occur in the 1960s, and especially in the 1970s and beyond.

Beach Drive-In Theater

While the official policy of the United States Air Force was to publicly deny the reality of UFOs, privately they expressed intense interest in the subject, particularly if the reports came from military personnel. Proof of this comes from the testimony of an anonymous Air Force 1st Lieutenant assigned to the 3300 Technical Training Group at Keesler Air Force Base in Mississippi. After seeing a UFO at the nearby Beach Drive-in Theater, the officer was interrogated by his superiors about what he saw. He was informed of his rights under Article 13 of the Uniform Code of Military Justice, and sworn under oath. The officer then voluntarily provided the following testimony:

"While attending the Beach Drive-In Theater on the night of 13 April [1952], I, First Lieutenant [redacted] and my wife, [redacted] sighted three unidentified objects in the sky out over the Gulf of Mexico, south of our location. The objects appeared to be in a formation or definite pattern, round in shape, and of a dull orange color similar to the glow of heated metal, and were traveling west. The objects appeared to be approximately thirty degrees in elevation. The objects were within my sight for approximately four to five seconds. After approximately three seconds, the objects appeared to change formation or alter their pattern, and then vanished to my right.

"I believe that the possibility of sighted objects being confused with falling stars is precluded by the direct horizontal path of the objects sighted and the difference in color between a star and the sighted objects."

While this sighting appears to be more of a random fly-by then a drive-in movie being targeted, it shows once again that drive-in movies are, at the very least, a good place to see a UFO.

Yuma Drive-In Theater

A mere two days after the above case, the Yuma Drive-In Theater in Yuma, Arizona was visited multiple times. On April 15, 1952, Kenneth Coffey and his wife were enjoying a movie at the theater when they saw something strange in the sky overhead. Six or seven objects, all a "dull gleaming white" scooted across the sky in a V-formation. They estimated that the objects were about two miles high. They moved swiftly and disappeared into the distance.

One day later, on April 16, 1952, Lieutenant Gerald Williams and his date, Sally Ann Diggs (the daughter of Colonel Edward R. Diggs, Commanding Officer of the Yuma Air Force Base,) sighted a UFO over the Yuma Drive-In. In this case, it was clear that the drive-in theater was being specifically targeted.

The sighting was initially kept quiet, however, twelve years afterward, Sally Ann Diggs reported it to investigators.

"No detail could be forgotten from that night in April 1952," writes Diggs. "It was a calm night, hot as usual for Yuma, Arizona. My date, Lieutenant Gerald Williams and I had gone to a drive-in movie. The movies started late due to the lack of darkness. The first feature was approximately one-half finished when I decided to get out of the car. An extremely bright light caught my eyes from an angle to the right side of the movie screen. The object which emitted the light was one of the most awe-inspiring sights I have ever seen. I stood looking, transfixed, for I had never seen anything like this.

"It was quite large, appearing to be the size of a car...It was beautiful in a weird way. The shape was that of two gently sloping bowls...each with rims to the other, and bottoms circular and flat. It almost seemed to be a portion of the landscape, for it was not very high in the sky, and its form was completely illuminated by its own lighting system. The top portion rotated ever so slowly, and I would not have noticed any movement if what may have been scars, indentions or some type of markings had not appeared and disappeared. It was possible that the lower portion moved also, but I did not feel that it did.

"The center rim or ring housed the yellow and rose-red pastel lights, which completely bathed the object in light...With all the car windows open and the volume of the car speakers on, it would be impossible to say for sure that there was no sound, but I do not believe that there was any. It merely sat there, and the top moved slowly.

"I called into the car for Gerry, and he too got out as soon as he saw my sighting. We stood by the car in absolute awe. Finally catching his breath, I recall him saying, 'I've never seen anything like that in my life. My God, it's huge.'

"As I leaned over and tried to tap the shoulder of the man in the next car, the object's lights became a pale, honest green, and the object moved steadily and smoothly up and down twice. I was sure it would come over the top of the cars, for it did appear to be something that could handle itself with ease. But instead, it veered to the right at a thirty-degree angle and in an extremely rapid time, it flew out of sight.

"I was speechless. And we got back to the car. Both of us were limp by that time."

Stunned, Diggs called out to the person in the car next to them, asking if he'd seen "the peculiar object up there."

The man replied that he had been watching the movie, and didn't see anything. "What was it you saw?" he asked.

"Just something odd," Diggs told him.

Both Diggs and Lt. Williams were amazed. "We began to realize then that something was very unusual," said Diggs. "And although Gerry was a pilot, we had neither seen anything shaped, colored or with speed such as this. We decided to leave for home at that point, and we went back to the hotel where my family had been staying...When we came in, my father asked if we had been in an accident. He said we were both white enough to have seen a ghost."

Diggs and Williams related what they had seen. Colonel Diggs immediately phoned Yuma AFB and demanded that they send someone over to investigate. Shortly later, an officer arrived from the base, and to their disappointment, attempted to explain away their sighting.

"The gentleman was obviously skeptical," says Diggs, "and took Lt. Williams's statement and my statement, in part, by longhand. He asked a few questions of us, but the whole vein was one of ridicule, as far as he dared with my father there. I do remember that he asked Lt. Williams why he was here, to which he replied that he was on leave from the Air Base in Portland, Oregon. The Public Information Officer asked him if he was on medical or R&R. He was not on either, but the insinuation was there, nevertheless. When the Captain was ready to leave, he told us all that it might be a good idea not to discuss the incident with anyone. He left us with the air that it wasn't top secret, but that it was a hallucination."

For the next three weeks, Diggs and Williams checked the local newspapers. There wasn't a single mention of what they had seen. Says Sally Ann Diggs, "...it does seem that something wasn't 'foul in Denmark,' but was foul in Yuma."

Years following the incident, researcher Richard Hall, working for NICAP, wrote to Colonel Edward R. Diggs, asking him to confirm the incident. Colonel Diggs confirmed the report and the date, and wrote, "As I did not observe the manifestation, there is little I can add, except to say that the sighting appeared to have caused quite a stir among those present at the drive-in theater at that time."

Incredibly, the encounters at Yuma Drive-In weren't over yet. On April 27, 1952, eleven days after the sighting by Diggs and Williams, there was another sighting at the drive-in. The witness in this case was an Air Force Sergeant and Chief of the Operating Location 1903-4 AACS Squadron at the Yuma County Airport.

Says the officer, "On the 27th of April 1952, between the hours of 8:30 and 10:30 p.m., my wife and I, while sitting in our automobile at the Yuma Drive-In Theater at Yuma, Arizona noticed what at first seemed to be falling stars, but upon following them we observed them to fly horizontal with the ground and then make a very definite abrupt change of altitude, disappearing in the clouds. Several minutes later two similar objects appeared flying parallel with each other. After a few seconds one continued straight ahead, the other veered sharply to the north and passed over the town of Yuma, disappearing into the clouds. All the objects sighted, which numbered seven or eight, were traveling from northeast to southeast, were round and emitted a fiery red glow. On one occasion after watching this particular object after it had made an abrupt change of altitude, it seemed as though it were a whirling disc."

The officer submitted his sighting to Project Blue Book officers. In his statement, he wrote, "Being a tower operator and being familiar with jet aircraft and other types, I am very sure it could not have been an aircraft or any other object that I have experience of seeing before. I have read about other reports on flying saucers or such as they are named and can very definitely state that their abrupt change of altitude was not normal, nor was their appearance."

Twenty-four years after this incident, the Yuma Drive-In theater would produce another startling sighting, making it perhaps the most UFO-frequented drive-in theater on record.

Universal City Drive-In Theater

Many of the witnesses of UFOs at drive-in theaters involve military officers. Obviously, this is not because military officers are the only ones who see UFOs, but rather because reporters and investigators viewed them as particularly reliable eyewitnesses.

This next case, which involves a dramatic display, comes from an Air Force Captain and member of the Physiology Branch of the Aero Medical Lab. After seeing a UFO at a drive-in theater in Universal City, Texas on May 21, 1952, the anonymous officer felt compelled to report his sighting officially. He was put in touch with officers at Project Blue Book, who prepared the following report describing the Captain's sighting:

"The objects were sighted for a period of one half-hour between 2100 and 2130 CST [9:00-9:30 p.m.,] from a drive-in theater located near Randolph AFB...The objects were noticed to the right of the screen. A total of about fifteen to twenty objects were observed. They were observed one at a time without more than three observations at once. They appeared to be about three times as bright as Venus, four times as fast as an F-86 [jet fighter], and about one-twentieth the size of a full moon. They were bright bluish-white in color. They were going back and forth, up and down, although most of them tended to go upward. One was noted to perform a nearly perfect S-shaped sine-wave. They would suddenly come into view and disappear. They did not gradually fade out. The weather was CAVU [clear and visibility unlimited.]"

Once again, the UFOs appear right next to the screen, and perform fantastic maneuvers for a long period of time. Clearly, they want to be seen.

Starlight Outdoor Theater

About one month later, at around 10:00 p.m., on July 17, 1952, Air Force Master Sergeant Gordon S. Anderson and his girlfriend, Lee Gerber, were at the Starlight Outdoor Theater in Rapid City, South Dakota when they observed two "V-formations" of orange-colored objects move overhead. Each formation contained about a dozen points of light. It was a clear and still night.

"The first appearance of these objects was over the air base," Anderson told the military investigators. "There were two V-type formations, one formation following the other. They resembled orange discs, and their estimated altitude was around 15,000 feet. They were traveling at a rate six or seven times the speed of a jet fighter."

Lee Gerber's testimony corroborated Anderson's. Said Gerber, "I observed this group of orange-colored objects after they were further south from where Sergeant Anderson first noticed them. They were traveling at a tremendous rate of speed."

After interviewing the witnesses, officials at the base said only that "Subject was not observed," claiming that nobody at the base saw the objects. They then said that anyone sighting "flying saucers" is required to report their sighting.

Writes researcher Loren Gross, "One would think that air base officials would be well aware of two formations of aircraft flying over the field at 10:00 in the evening. Apparently, no such thing took place, so that explanation was not suggested."

Six Drive-In Theater Encounters

In the summer of 1952, a massive UFO wave swept across the United States. The objects often appeared at night, usually in small groups. Once again, drive-in theaters proved to be an ideal location to view a UFO. While a few cases might involve theaters that are being targeted, in most the witnesses are simply in the right place at the right time. A few cases might fall under either category. Consider the following six drive-in UFO encounters, all of which took place the last week of July 1952.

The first two cases both took place on the same evening, but in different parts of the United States. While both these cases involve dramatic maneuvers, it's difficult to say if the theaters themselves have been targeted.

On the evening of July 22, 1952, Nicholas Jacobson was at the Fresh Pond Drive-In Theater in Newton, Massachusetts, when he saw four or five bright star-like objects approaching overhead. Says Jacobson, "What got me about them was that after watching them pass in a straight line, just parallel to my vision, to the line of the picture screen against the sky, two of them slowed down, turned and shot up out of sight. It's a peculiar thing to see. You can hardly believe it when it's happening."

Incidentally, the theater was large enough to hold more than 1000 cars. No word on if there were other witnesses to Jacobson's sighting.

At 10:50 p.m., on the same evening, Eric Smith was at a drive-in theater in Portales, New Mexico. Suddenly his attention was drawn away from the movie screen to a cluster of high-flying lights in a V-formation. The objects moved very quickly, traveling from horizon to horizon in about four seconds. To Smith's surprise, after reaching the horizon, the formation of objects "reversed positions like a Notre Dame backfield." They then zoomed to the northeast, maneuvering in a curving arc of about seventy-five degrees.

Both of these cases involve fantastic maneuvers, but the sightings were brief and involved high altitude objects. Most cases of targeted theaters are low altitude sightings that last more than a few seconds. The next four cases (like the two above) do not appear to involve targeted theaters. Instead, the last week of July 1952 proved to be a fortuitous time to be outside at night and see a UFO.

Two days later and just sixteen miles away from Portales, on the evening of July 24, 1952, Captain J.W. Titus of the 1404 Fighter Bomber Wing at Clovis Air Force Base in Clovis, New Mexico, was viewing a film at the local drive-in theater when he saw two "oval-shaped objects" about three or four miles high, moving east at about 400 to 600 mph. Once they reached the edge of the horizon, they made an eighty-degree turn and moved off to the north and out of view. Titus said that the objects had a "reddish-orange neon glow" and "seemed to float through the air as a ball travels through water when pulled with a string."

Three days later, on the evening of July 27, 1952, Air Force Major Freeman (a Wing Communications Officer of the 11th Strategic Wing) was with two other women at a drive-in theater in Spokane, Washington. All three witnesses, and several other people at the drive-in were amazed to see about a dozen brilliant white lights move in a "loose formation" heading north to south. Although many people in the theater must have observed the objects, Major Williams was apparently the only witness to file an official report.

Meanwhile, movie-goers at another nearby drive-in theater on the other side of town also saw the objects, describing them as luminous white discs, or "clay pigeons." The objects came from the northeast and vanished behind the movie screen. Reports then surfaced that other witnesses had also seen UFOs from the same drive-in "somewhat earlier."

Three days after that, at 8:00 p.m., on July 30, 1952, numerous movie-goers at the Sedalia Drive-In Theater in Sedalia, Missouri sat in their cars and prepared to watch a movie. During the film, a reddish, glowing, disc-like object appeared overhead, moving from west to east. The object remained in view for an estimated eight minutes. It was in a vertical position, and as it passed directly over the drive-in, the witnesses saw a clear sideview of the object. It was totally silent.

After it left, some witnesses were skeptical that it was a genuine UFO, while others were thoroughly convinced that they had seen something unexplained. Reporters from the local newspaper, the *Capital*, heard about the sighting and interviewed some of the witnesses. The account appeared in the newspaper the next day, under the headline: "Feature Attraction at the Drive-In Is Not a Movie."

Almost seventy years later, the Sedalia Drive-In is still in operation.

Terrace Drive-In Theater

A particularly dramatic drive-in UFO encounter occurred at 10:30 p.m., on August 12, 1952. This case is a perfect example of a UFO putting on a clear display and showing itself off.

Lieutenant Jenkins of the Navy Reserve was enjoying a drive-in movie with more than a hundred other people at the Terrace Drive-In Theatre off Highway 99 in Bakersfield, California. The theater had space for 650 cars.

Jenkins sat in his 1950 Cadillac near the left-center, toward the back of the lot. The movie was playing when he suddenly noticed "two lights" moving "as fast as a jet," northeast at about 2000 feet altitude, from the left side of the screen.

To his surprise, the object suddenly stopped directly above the screen. It was lit up like a Christmas tree, the lieutenant said, and was in full view of all the theater-goers, all who saw the object. The object was so low and obvious, said Jenkins, that nobody could fail to notice it.

After stopping momentarily, the object executed a quick ninety-degree turn to the southeast, then accelerated in a sharp climb and passed out of sight.

Jenkins and all the other theater-goers were shocked. Jenkins immediately called the local police station, as apparently did other witnesses.

Meanwhile, back at the Kern County Sheriff's Department in Bakersfield, Deputy Sheriff Leroy Hatfield picked up the phone and talked to Lt. Jenkins, who excitedly informed him about the UFO which had buzzed the Terrace Drive-In.

Sheriff Hatfield took Jenkins' testimony, and hung up the phone, which immediately began ringing again. It was another person from the drive-in calling to report the same thing that Jenkins had seen. Several calls came after that, all from patrons of the Terrace Drive-In Theater reporting the UFO.

Due to the large number of calls, Sheriff Hatfield had no choice but to get in his police cruiser and drive to the scene to investigate for himself.

Upon arrival, he was shocked to see more than a hundred people still at the theater, talking about what they had seen. Dozens of people immediately besieged Hatfield, telling him about the low-level sighting.

Hatfield took statements from at least twenty-three witnesses, at which point, he had to give his arm a rest. He estimates that there were at least eighty other people there who he could have interviewed. After interviewing about one-third of them, he was able to obtain enough descriptions to get a pretty good idea of what people had seen.

Lt. Jenkins said the object had a brightly lit window on the frontside, and a dim blue-orange light on the rear.

The other witnesses provided similar descriptions. One said the UFO appeared as a "triangular-shaped object, brownish in color, larger than an airliner, surrounded by dim lights."

Another said it "looked like a zeppelin that was lit up faintly with lights around the sides."

One witness said that the object "appeared oblong and had a group of six lights surrounding it."

One said the object was "long, slender, hazy, possibly orange color."

Yet another said the UFO "appeared to be a lot of little glows around in a circle, at about a hundred feet of altitude."

Still another said it was "crescent-shaped [and] dimly lit."

One witness said it was "one big object with six or seven lights..."

Each description varied slightly, particularly regarding its shape, but all agreed that it was very low, totally silent, covered with lights and was definitely not a plane.

Says researcher Loren Gross, "Whatever it was, it was a real show-stopper...we may never know what it was that buzzed the Terrace Drive-In that night."

Immediately following the incident, officer Leroy Hatfield called the Air Force to report the sighting. An officer at Edwards

Air Force Base took the call and forwarded it to Project Blue Book officers, who took his testimony and wrote up a report.

The military apparently found Hatfield's report to be of extreme interest. On August 13, 1952, Hatfield's testimony was forwarded to the Air Technical Intelligence Command Center (ATIC) at Wright-Patterson Air Force Base in Dayton, Ohio, Ent AFB in Colorado Springs, Colorado, and finally to the Director of Intelligence at Washington DC.

The document, marked "ACTION," is one and a half pages long, and reads, in part, "...a large object passed over an operating drive-in theater in Bakersfield, California, and was witnessed by thirty to forty persons. The following is the consensus of impressions -- the object was larger than a four-engine airliner, was dark and seen only in the light reflected from the movie screen. It was adjudged to be 200 to 300 feet off the ground, traveling slowly northeast at sixty mph and was without sound of motive power. It was reported to appear as a 'V'-shaped object, colored brown, and had what appeared to be a ring of light around it that seemed to disappear when it had passed across the drive-in."

This case shows once again that the U.S. government was closely monitoring UFO activity across the world, including at drive-in theaters.

Rodeo Drive-In Theater

Only one day later, the UFOs appeared over another drive-in theater. Air Force Reserve Captain Stanley W. Thompson (an engineer employed at Edwards Air Force Base) was with his wife, son and nephew at the Rodeo Drive-In Theater in Tucson, Arizona. It was precisely 11:10 p.m., on August 13, 1952.

All four of them were watching the movie when they saw a group of lights in the distance. Stanley saw them first and immediately alerted his family. The objects appeared to be accelerating and coming closer. "As they became more distinct," said Stanley, "I could see definite symmetry and make out individual lights."

The objects moved swiftly, passing overhead and disappearing over the opposite horizon in only about five seconds. Stanley was unsure whether the objects were high up and very large, or as low as 1000 feet and fairly small.

"I had always hoped that if I saw any of these things," said Stanley, "I would be able to make all kinds of observations, such as whether they obscured a star when passing overhead. But there was just no time for that."

This report appears to be a lucky chance sighting. By now it's clear that drive-in encounters fall into two main categories: random coincidental fly-bys, (like this case) and intentionally targeted theaters. The second category involves encounters that are typically long-lasting, low-level, close-up sightings with UFOs that behave in ways that make it obvious they want to be seen. And as the years passed, these types of cases began to increase in frequency.

Family Drive-In Theater

The early 1950s were an extremely active time for drive-in movie encounters. It appears that the UFO occupants were pursuing an aggressive agenda of making themselves known. Only two days after the above incident, at around 9:45 p.m., on August 15, 1952, a lieutenant colonel, his wife, and their two children experienced a dramatic encounter at the Family Drive-In Theater in Urbana, Illinois. They were watching the movie and first noticed the object when it was about seventy degrees above the horizon. It was a reddish-green glowing light and appeared several times larger than a star.

As they watched the strange light, it dropped down and made a sudden ninety-degree turn. It then traveled at high speed, disappearing over the horizon. It was in view for only about five seconds, but long enough for the colonel and his family to determine that it was not a plane or conventional aircraft. No sound was heard coming from the object.

On the very same evening, at around 9:00 p.m., Henry Broome and his wife were at the West Gate Drive-In Theater in West Palm Beach, Florida when they saw an object move over the theater. They described it as looking "like two pie pans put together, rounded at the back."

Corral & Western Drive-In Theaters

In August 1951, the city of Lubbock, Texas experienced a UFO sighting that made national headlines. Exactly one year later, in August 1952, another wave of sightings swept through the small town. The UFOs were particularly brazen, showing themselves to large groups of people, including at two separate drive-in movie theaters in the same town. One evening around 9:00 - 10:00 p.m., in late August 1952, Frank Hoenig and his wife were enjoying a movie at the Corral Drive-In Theater in Lubbock when they saw mysterious "spots of light" traveling "very fast" at high altitude overhead. Other witnesses at the theater also observed the strange lights.

A few days later, also around 9:00 - 10:00 p.m., a couple (who insisted upon anonymity) were at the Western Drive-In Theater, where they observed two flights of objects described as "slightly oblong" and moving with a speed that was "out of this world." Another couple at the theater also saw the objects and described them as a "string of blueish lights traveling from north to south."

Ironically, during these sightings, the indoor movie theater in Lubbock was featuring the classic science fiction film, *The Thing from Another World*. Meanwhile, at the same time, those outside at the city drive-ins were actually seeing a *thing* from another world!

El Cajon Drive-In Theater

The UFO wave of 1952 remains one of the biggest in United States history. Edward Ruppelt of Project Blue Book wrote that "during a six-month period in 1952, 148 of the world's leading newspapers carried a total of 16,000 items about UFOs."

Meanwhile, drive-in UFO encounters occurred across the United States on a nearly weekly basis. As the number of cases grows, it becomes increasingly apparent that there is a connection between UFOs and drive-in theaters.

On August 16, 1952, at around 11:00 p.m., audience members of the El Cajon Drive-In Theater in El Cajon, California saw a veritable fleet of objects.

Mrs. Charles Chinell observed a V-formation of at least twenty-four "orange-colored" lights moving at jet speed from north to south.

Another witness at the theater described the formation of lights as looking "like a flying saucer with twenty or thirty portholes."

Are these chance sightings? Were the witnesses in the right place at the right time to see a UFO? Were the UFO occupants aware that they were being observed?

While any answer is impossible to prove, the extraordinarily high levels of activity during the year of 1952 do show that the UFOs had little fear of being observed. While the El Cajon theater may not have been specifically targeted, the UFO that flew over the theater was not afraid of being seen.

Yucca Drive-In Theater

This next case is another solid example of a drive-in theater being specifically targeted for a UFO display.

On the evening of September 9, 1952, numerous movie-goers at the Yucca Drive-In Theater in Gallup, New Mexico enjoyed "an added feature" above and beyond the regular showing. Among the many witnesses was Eddie Bowman, who said that the object first appeared just before the end of the last show. It was a bright glowing object, and was, he said, "about the size of a car's headlight."

He first thought it was a shooting star until it zoomed close to the ground, leveled off mere feet above the ground, and then gained altitude again as it moved off toward the west. Other patrons at the theater described the same incredible maneuver. "I wouldn't have believed it if I hadn't seen it," Bowman told reporters. "But I saw it. And the management admitted it was not on the regular program."

While low-level UFO sightings are not rare, it is unusual for UFOs to come within feet of the ground in front of a large group of witnesses. With drive-in encounters, however, this type of behavior is the norm.

Curiously, the United States Geological Survey took an aerial photograph of this particular drive-in only four days following the sighting. The Yucca Drive-In (which could hold 249 cars) was located along the now famous Route 66. Like most drive-in theaters from the 1950s, it is no longer in operation.

Albuquerque & Biloxi Drive-In Theaters

One curious feature of drive-in movie encounters is the tendency of the UFOs to appear right next to the screen, exactly where the audience is looking, such as this next case.

It was just after 10:00 p.m., on September 14, 1952, and Milton Klassen (a senior in geology at the University of New Mexico) was with a friend at the Albuquerque Drive-In when they both saw a pair of "flying saucers." Klassen said the objects appeared just above the movie screen, and looked like "yellowish platter-shaped lights."

He and his friend were amazed. "For four or five seconds the objects weaved back and forth and seemed to play with each other," said Klassen. "Then they disappeared."

On the same evening that Milton Klassen and others were observing UFOs dancing over the Albuquerque Drive-In, movie-goers at another drive-in theater in Biloxi, Mississippi were also treated to a remarkable display. Starting around 9:10 p.m., people at the theater noticed a cigar-shaped, greenish-white object which was so unusual in appearance that people in the audience stopped watching the movie and instead turned their attention to the sky. The object, which hovered in the eastern sky, began to dim in brightness and then seemed to change shape from a cigar to a semi-circle, at which point it climbed straight up and moved out of view.

Five minutes later, another identical-looking object appeared in the same spot, glowing brighter and brighter. It remained in place for nearly one hour at which time it suddenly "broke up" and disappeared.

A third object now appeared, slightly higher and further east. This object remained in place until at least 11:00 p.m., at which time, the movie ended and the theater-goers left the scene.

September 1952 turned out to be a very active month. About two weeks later, audience members at the Woomera West Open-Air Theatre in Woomera, South Australia were treated to a quick fly-by. Witnesses said the object was silent, with two brightly-lit portholes, and cylindrical or cigar-shaped. Incidentally, the Woomera area is known to be a location of secret government testing in avionics and rocketry.

Star-Lite Drive-In Theater

The year of 1952 remains the most prolific in terms of drive-in theater encounters. A particularly credible account comes from an anonymous 2nd lieutenant (also an aeronautical engineer) assigned to the missile test unit at Holloman AFB. On October 7, 1952, the officer and his wife were at the Star-Lite Drive-In Theater in Alamogordo, New Mexico when they both saw something that they were unable to explain.

Says the officer, "...my wife called my attention to a light that appeared to be in the sky through our windshield. It looked oval in shape, the major axis being almost vertical, and about a third of a thumb's length in height, the hand being held out at arm's length. It was lighter on the ridge edge and top than it was in the center and left side, and seemed to be a whitish or pale-blue in color."

The object first appeared in the east, then moved in a straight line about twenty degrees above the horizon, becoming gradually dimmer until it faded out "all in a very short length of time."

This case lacks the earmark features of a targeted encounter, and appears to be a random fly-by. And to be fair, this area of New Mexico was a magnet of UFO activity, perhaps because of the nuclear research and missile testing taking place at nearby Holloman and White Sands AFB.

Whatever the case, it was around this time that the incredible wave of 1952 came to an end. If the public hadn't known about UFOs before 1952, they did now.

Greenfield Drive-In Theater

With the close of 1952, and a lessening number of UFO reports, drive-in theater encounters slowed dramatically. Instead of appearing every couple of weeks or so, UFOs targeted theaters an average of about one per year. For whatever reason, the UFOs were changing their tactics.

On the evening of October 2, 1953, visitors at a drive-in theater in Greenfield, Massachusetts were enjoying the movie when they suddenly noticed a very-strange looking object moving overhead. Several people in the parking lot saw the object and described its appearance as a "badminton bird" or a "glowing red cigar." It was in view for only a few seconds as it traversed the sky and disappeared behind the movie screen.

Over the past two months, there had been other sightings in the area. In July, two residents saw an object hovering, turning at right angles and zooming at high speed for a period of about fifteen minutes. In August, two other witnesses saw a small unidentified orb of light hovering at treetop level at the north edge of town.

Clearly just a fly-by, cases like this one might not seem as compelling as those in which theaters are directly targeted. They do still, however, provide an extra attraction that indoor movie theaters will never be able to offer. And in most cases, the witnesses are impressed enough to become believers in UFOs.

Skyline Drive-In Theater

Among the most important and influential cases in this book is an event that took place on July 17, 1954 at the Skyline Drive-In Theater in St. Louis, Missouri. Built in 1950, it was a fairly large theater, with a capacity of 600 cars. It was located next to a small airport.

The main witness was, at the time, a six and a half-year-old boy by the name of Peter Davenport. His father worked for the local airlines, and his mother's family included a few fighter pilots. As a result, Peter had developed a strong interest in aircraft. "I prided myself on my ability to see and to identify almost any type of aircraft you could imagine," he says.

On that night, Peter, his older brother, and their mother decided to go to the drive-in. "I was seated in the right-hand seat of our 1953 Studebaker with a chrome ring on the nose," he says.

They were enjoying the movie when, as Peter says, "a disturbance started brewing in the theater. People started shouting and running around, and staring up at the sky. And I looked out the right-hand side of the car, and saw one of the most dramatic bizarre-looking things I've ever seen in my life.

"It was bright red, the color of a red traffic signal, with perhaps just a shade of orange in it...It was casting a red light all over the theater, all over the airport, as far as we could see."

The object had the apparent size of a full moon, but was more oval in shape. "It was shaped like an eye," Peter says, "or like the CBS logo, and it was hovering almost motionless in the sky...stopped, almost stock-still, in the sky east of our location."

Unknown to Peter and his family, his own father was in the St. Louis Airport tower, and along with several other people, was viewing the object through binoculars.

Meanwhile, the audience at the theater grew increasingly agitated. "Everyone at the theater saw it," Peter says. "And they were getting out of their vehicles, standing, seemingly mesmerized by this image before them."

Peter isn't sure how many minutes the object remained in place, but it wasn't long. As he says, "People were getting out of their cars, gesticulating, pointing, and actually running toward it. In a matter of seconds, it accelerated and was gone over the horizon...It went from about 100 degrees relative to the centerline of the car, to going over the northwestern horizon from a dead stop in about two or three seconds."

Once the object was gone, the conversation at the theater exploded. "It was a dramatic, dramatic event," Peter says. "Everybody was flummoxed by it."

For Peter, the sighting was to have lifelong consequences. "That was no aircraft from this planet," Peter says. "Whatever I saw that day at that drive-in theater was something very unusual. And I think it's fair to say that I've been entranced by the UFO phenomenon ever since."

Forty years later, Peter still maintained a strong interest in UFOs. While he didn't actively investigate UFO cases, he was good friends with a very active and respected UFO investigator by the name of Bob Gribble.

Knowing that many people who encountered UFOs had no idea who to call about it. Gribble decided to take action. Years earlier, in 1974, he founded a little organization called the National UFO Reporting Center. He set up a 24-hour telephone hotline. He coordinated with police departments and put out limited ads.

Soon the calls began to flood in. Before long, Gribble had collected a database of UFO reports from every state in the United States, and from many countries across the world.

Twenty years later, in 1994, the workload became too heavy. Unable to find anybody willing to take over, he was about to close down the organization.

When Peter Davenport heard the news, he volunteered to take over. Gribble warned him that it was a lot of work, but Peter said he was committed to making it a success.

Peter soon realized what he had gotten himself into. The organization is entirely non-profit and self-funded. It was a lot of work, and often thankless. If he had known how hard it would be, he says, he might have made another choice.

But ultimately, he was encouraged by the many grateful responses he has received from thankful witnesses who had nowhere else to turn.

The NUFORC database has now grown to over a hundred thousand cases, with the number of reports escalating each year. It has become one of the leading civilian UFO reporting and research organizations in the entire world.

Peter, who has a degree from Stanford University, has now been the director of NUFORC for more than twenty-five years.

"What originally got me involved in UFOs," says Davenport, "was [the] very dramatic sighting I had as a young boy...It was at that point that I was committed to becoming the director of the National UFO Reporting Center. It looks to me, and it first became apparent to me from that sighting, that we are dealing with something that is not manufactured on this planet. The reason I'm the director of the National UFO Reporting Center is because of that sighting in 1954."

Two years following his sighting, the Skyline Drive-In Theater was struck by lightning during a showing and burned to the ground. It was quickly rebuilt, but closed down one year later.

Lakeshore Drive-In Theater

As we have seen, not all cases involve theaters being targeted. Because witnesses are outside at night, their chances of seeing a UFO are significantly increased. This next case provides a good example of being in the right place at the right time to see a UFO.

It was a clear evening around 9:30 p.m., on August 21, 1954, and "Riley" was at the Lakeshore Drive-In Theater in Denver, Colorado. Looking up, he saw ten or twelve dim red fluorescent-looking lights moving in formation overhead. He was unable to determine if they were separate objects, or were lights attached to a single massive object. Whatever the "thing" was, it moved almost directly overhead very quickly from east to west at a very high altitude. The objects traveled from horizon to horizon in about three or four seconds.

Riley was an Air Force pilot and had logged about 3000 hours of flying time during World War II. He was familiar with aircraft, but was unable to identify what he saw. He estimates that the UFO moved at a speed of about 5000 to 6000 mph. One month later, on September 17, Special Agent Chester A. Cummins from the Air Force Office of Special Investigations (OSI) interviewed Riley, expressing great interest in what he had seen.

With a capacity of 1000 cars, there were likely other witnesses.

Fort Wayne Drive-In Theater

In some cases, the UFOs are at such a low elevation, it seems impossible to come to any other conclusion than that the UFOs want to be seen.

In the summer of 1955, nine-year-old Alan (pseudonym) and his brother were at a drive-in theater in Fort Wayne, Indiana. Their mother and step-father were in the front seat when four "silver discs" appeared on the horizon, heading in their direction.

"The discs approached from our left front," Alan says, "continued almost directly overhead, and disappeared into the distance behind our right rear. As they neared our location, we all exited the car and watched them pass overhead. They were moving slowly and skittered about erratically, though staying in a rough formation, and moving along a straight route. They made no sound...Everyone at the movie was standing outside their cars watching. When they were overhead, they appeared to be no more than 200 feet above us and perhaps 100 feet in diameter."

The objects were saucer-shaped and had what appeared to be portholes. The next day, the local newspaper, the *Journal Gazette*, printed a story about the sighting. Using the information from people who called in, they were able to track the speed and direction of the objects as they moved over Fort Wayne.

Years later, Alan still remembered the sighting vividly, and recognizing its importance, he submitted a formal report to MUFON.

Pratt Drive-In Theater

If UFOs are truly showing themselves over drive-in theaters in an attempt to announce their presence and generate interest in the subject, then the UFO occupants must surely be pleased by the results of this next case.

It was 8:30 p.m., on May 8, 1956 at the Pratt Drive-In Theater in Pratt, Kansas, when numerous people watching the movie saw four luminous saucer-shaped objects flying in formation overhead. The witnesses phoned the Ground Observer Corps (GOC) who also observed the objects from their observation post. The Air Force witnesses described the objects as "glowing pink with shadings of orange and green."

In an apparent coincidence, (or not!) the premiere of the documentary film, "UFO," was airing at the Fox Wilshire Theater in Beverly Hills, California the next day. When the film aired, more than 400 people showed up to view the movie, which was far more people than the theater owners had been expecting. Apparently public interest in UFOs was growing fast. The ETs' agenda of making their presence known was showing definite signs of success.

Florence Drive-In Theater

All across the United States, people at drive-in theaters continued to see UFOs.

On the evening of September 9, 1956, several people at the 700-car-capacity Florence Drive-in Theater in Florence, Kentucky discovered that, as one reporter said, "the best show was not on screen, but in the dark sky." They were watching the movie when a conventional plane passed overhead and began circling. Weirdly, the plane was being trailed by a "strange light." After following the plane for a brief time, the "mystery light" suddenly zoomed away.

Then another airplane moved overhead, also being followed by an "unknown pursuer." Like the first object, the UFO trailed the plane for several moments, and then suddenly accelerated and passed the plane at high speed. One witness at the drive-in, Jack Juely, told reporters that the sighting was "the most unusual I've ever seen."

The UFOs' behavior of pursuing planes once again echoes the brazen audacity of the occupants. Whether it's chasing planes through the sky, pacing cars down highways, or hovering over drive-in theaters, UFOs seem to be putting on some sort of publicity campaign.

Oakville Drive-In Theater

The vast majority of drive-in theater encounters occur in the United States, with only a few outside the country, such as the following.

On the evening of July 23, 1957, movie-goers at a drive-in theater in Oakville, Ontario, in Canada, saw a group of three high-flying glowing objects pass over the theater during the movie. Two friends, Robert Guertin and Richard Beresford were watching the movie when Guertin suddenly saw something strange overhead. "I glanced up," Guertin said, "and I saw three light-bluish lights flying in a westerly direction."

Guertin immediately called out to his friend, Richard, and the two of them observed the UFOs. "As we watched, they made a lazy turn to the south. It took them about two minutes to cross the sky. We told a man and his wife sitting in the next car, and they saw them also."

Guertin was a former Air Cadet with ground observer training. He estimated that the objects moved at a speed of at least 1000 mph. He had read about flying saucers in the newspaper, but, as he says, "This was the first time I have ever seen them. It gives you quite a jolt."

The next evening, on July 24, the Oakville police station was "flooded" with calls from local residents reporting flying saucers over the town. Each caller said the objects were blue-white and flying very high in the sky. Some saw only one object, while others saw two or three. A few said that the objects emitted a "whirring" sound as they passed overhead.

Piedmont Drive-In Theater

In this next case, UFOs targeted both a school and a nearby drive-in theater on the same night.

At 7:20 p.m., on September 26, 1957, five students at Agnes Scott College in Atlanta, Georgia were out on the campus when they saw a strange object with three searchlights pass overhead. "We couldn't hear it until it was directly over us," said Mary Hammond, one of the student witnesses at the school. Fifty minutes later, at 8:10 p.m., the object returned and made another pass over the school. Hammond was unable to determine the exact shape of the object, but due to the arrangement of the lights, she guessed it might have been delta-shaped.

Fifty minutes later, at 9:00 p.m., the object was back, this time over the Piedmont Drive-In Theater, where it was seen by about a dozen theater patrons. With room for 650 cars, the actual number of witnesses may have been much higher. One of them was Homer Elzey, a marshal from Fulton County. "It came right over the parking area of the Piedmont Drive-In Theater, and it looked very high up," said Elzey. He wasn't sure how high up the object was, but said it looked about the size of a "grapefruit" and moved as quick as lightning.

Another witness at the theater, Walter Marx, said that as the object passed overhead, it suddenly stopped, turned a bright beam of light downward, and then resumed its flight, disappearing off into the distance.

Reporters for the *Atlanta Constitution* newspaper heard about the sighting and after interviewing the witnesses, contacted the Atlanta Municipal Airport and Dobbins Air Force Base. Both denied seeing anything unusual or receiving any reports.

Three Way Drive-In Theater

One week after the above sighting, at 9:15 p.m., on November 3, 1957, numerous people at the Three Way Drive-In Theater, in Clifton, Arizona stopped watching the film and instead turned their attention to a round, silver-colored, disc-shaped object in the sky overhead.

Larry Parsons (age sixteen) was among the many witnesses and said it moved at a "terrific" rate of speed. "It came across the horizon, crossed to the west, went through a cloud and disappeared over the horizon," he said. Another person at the drive-in, Mary Chapman, gave an identical description.

Other people nearby the theater also saw the object. Five minutes after it was seen at the Three Way Drive-In, three deer hunters driving near Clifton saw a "silver-colored object...like two hubcaps together" move very quickly across the sky.

It does not appear that the theater was specifically targeted in this instance. Perhaps significant is the fact that Clifton is a mining town adjacent to Morenci, Arizona. Morenci contains a large copper smelting plant and there are many copper mines in the area. These locations have all experienced numerous low-level UFO sightings. The theater is only eight miles away.

Perhaps of interest, the Three Way Drive-In earned its unusual name because it is located at the convergence of Highways 8, 78 and 191. While the screen and concession stand still stand, the theater is no longer operational.

King Center Twin Drive-In Theater

Again, in a number of cases, drive-in theaters are not necessarily targeted, but instead prove to be an ideal place to view a UFO. While these cases aren't as dramatic as the targeted cases, they are still of interest as they show how truly busy the decade of the 1950s was in terms of UFO activity.

Around 6:25 p.m., on November 6, 1957, Mrs. Grace D. Lester was at the King Center Twin Drive-In Theater in Houston, Texas watching the feature film when she saw a very strange object zigzagging overhead. It looked like an oversized extremely bright star-like object. She watched it for a few brief moments as it charged an "irregular" course across the sky and then disappeared.

Lester reported her sighting to the local newspapers and learned that there were many other witnesses to activity in the area that night, including six police officers.

The King Center Twin had twin screens and a capacity to hold 600 cars. Likely there were many other witnesses.

Waterford Drive-In Theater

One of the great things about drive-in UFO encounters, from an investigative standpoint, is that the UFOs are not only seen at a very low elevation, they are viewed by multiple witnesses, often for long periods of time. This makes it very difficult to dismiss the sightings as hoaxes, hallucinations or misperceptions.

And for every "lucky chance" sighting, there's another where the UFOs target the theater and put on a deliberate show for the witnesses, such as this next incredible case.

It was dusk, around 7:50 p.m., on August 18, 1959 at the Waterford Drive-In Theater in Waterford, Michigan. The sky wasn't quite dark yet as Wanda Bierl and her husband, Kenneth sat in their car waiting for the double feature movie to start. Playing on the screens that night were the two films, *Alias Jesse James* and *All Mine to Give*. Their three young children were playing at the drive-in playground at the front of the theater.

Says Wanda, "Suddenly my husband told me to look at those two things on the lower horizon."

Wanda looked where he was pointing. "There were two yellow discs in the sky, not in the heavens, but in our own atmosphere," she said. "The two objects faced each other and for about eight minutes, they stood perfectly still, except for when you looked at them very closely, they looked like they were driving with the wind and moving slightly. They moved separately and of their own accord. There wasn't a cloud in the sky...for about the next three minutes, one moved higher than the other, and they stood there drifting in place...We saw the people in other cars watching too, and some got out of their cars to look.

"All of a sudden, the lower one took off in a straight upward movement and became a very thin disc with a long yellow tail with a bit of red to it, making it look like a fire streak. Then thirty seconds later, the second one moved up and over and down in a perfect arc, leaving a yellow trail behind it.

"It disappeared completely while the first disc continued to go straight up, then leveled off and began flying perfectly straight for about three minutes, trailing to the right with a stream of yellowish-reddish vapor that faded to pink as it disappeared.

"As the first one faded, the second flying object came back into view and looked like it was coming straight at us, right under the other one, which reappeared again. They both arched together, like they were making a big U-turn and streaked away for the last time. The objects had very distinct lines, except when they moved in a blurred flight. They were very distinct in their movements, not like something just falling to earth. We were agog. It was unbelievable. There was a human intelligence about the whole thing...or superhuman."

The Bierls and other witnesses reported their sighting to newspapers. The next day, an article describing the incident appeared in the *Pontiac Press* under the headlines: "Flying Discs Seen in Area: Give Bonus Show at Drive-In."

Your Drive-In Theater

Some cases, such as the following fly-by, are sparse on details and not particularly dramatic. However, in contrast, they show just how special and unique the actual targeted encounters are.

On June 20, 1960, at around 10:40 p.m., Mrs. Robert Dahl was sitting in her car at the Your Drive-In Theater in Longview, Washington when she saw a large, fast-moving object. She first noticed it because it had a "peculiar glow." She observed it move quickly from west to east in the southern sky, before disappearing off into the distance. On that evening, multiple other residents in the area also reported strange activity.

Again, this appears to be another lucky chance sighting. As we shall soon see, however, these simple fly-bys are far out-numbered by the more dramatic targeted encounters. In fact, as the 1960s and 1970s progressed, the UFO occupants would become much braver, and would start putting on increasingly fantastic displays that made the encounters from the 1950s look like child's play.

Newington Drive-In Theater

It was around 11:30 p.m., on November 12, 1960 when a young couple, Richard Villa (21) and his girlfriend, Judith L. Fraser (19) were at a drive-in theater in Newington, Connecticut watching the movie, *The House of Usher*. The film had just reached a very exciting and suspenseful scene when the young couple noticed something in the sky above them even more interesting than the movie. It was a whole fleet of UFOs.

Says Fraser, "They were bright orange and looked as though they might be large, although their height made them look small...there were about a dozen, in a V-formation, with a line of them off to the side, heading from north to south."

Fraser saw them first, then pointed them out to her companion, who also saw them. "They came by just as there was a lot of action on the screen," Fraser said.

The objects were in view for only a few moments, disappearing from view behind the screen. After they were gone, the young couple went back to watching the movie. Later they reported their sighting to the local newspaper.

Tillicum Drive-In Theater

Are the UFOs showing themselves to the theater-goers on purpose, or by coincidence? Before you answer, consider this next dramatic UFO display.

One summer evening around 1961, "Brian" and his girlfriend decided to see a movie at the Tillicum Drive-in Theater in Victoria, Canada. During the film, two glowing, orange objects appeared above and to the left of the screen. At first, they seemed to be very high up. But over the next thirty minutes, they became bigger and brighter. By the time forty minutes had passed, the objects were so bright that the street lights began to go out, and it was impossible to watch the movie.

"By this time," says Brian, "I and many, many others that were at the outdoor theater were out of their cars, watching the two objects."

After a few moments, the objects moved upward, again taking almost twenty minutes to complete the maneuver, becoming smaller and dimmer, and eventually stopping exactly where they first appeared. While it was now dark enough to watch the film, the objects were not moving away.

Then the show began, and it wasn't on the movie screen. Says Brian, "They sat there for maybe another ten minutes, when one of the objects left the other, going across the sky in a zigzag movement, a back and forth motion...I remember watching it go behind us, all of which took at least five full minutes. My girlfriend at the time wouldn't even get out of the vehicle. I got back in [the car] to watch the show again, and I could still see the remaining object, still quite bright, watching the show."

After about ten minutes, the object suddenly shot in the opposite direction. "I remember it leaving in the blink of an eye," Brian says. "All you could see was a small streak in the direction it went. I'm sure there had to be fifty to sixty people that were out of their vehicles at that time, because there was no show to watch but that one. Funny thing too, I watched the newspapers and listened to the radio for many days, and nothing was ever said about that incident that I could ever find."

Charlottetown Drive-In Theater

Next to the United States, Canada is the second-leading producer of drive-in UFO encounters. This next case comes from Charlottetown, Prince Edward Island in Canada. While the sighting reported by the primary witness didn't take place over a drive-in, it appears that the object had recently visited one nearby, and not just once, but repeatedly.

"In the early 1960s, I had a UFO sighting not far from my home," says the anonymous witness. "I was about eighteen [years old] and on my way home about 11:30 p.m., when I happened to look up in the sky and spotted a round disk with flashing colored lights. It descended to about 200 feet and stopped as if observing me. I was the only one around this spot to witness this UFO so I have nobody else to talk to about it. I watched it for about one to two minutes and then it started to ascend upward first very slowly and then it sped up (not so fast that I could not watch it) to a distance where I still could make out its flashing lights and stopped and then (wow) this thing took off on a forty-five degree angle and within a couple of seconds it was gone. I stood there with my mouth open and said to myself -- *What was that thing?* Around this time there was a drive-in theatre not far from our home. There were a lot of UFO sightings around this drive-in theatre for a number of days. The newspaper in our city even advertised, 'Come to the drive-in and see the UFOs.'"

Like many people who have close-up sightings, the witness was left forever changed. As he says, "To this day I am convinced what I saw was no military aircraft or anything I could explain that could do what it did. I still star gaze out in the country away from the city lights hoping to see again what I saw some forty plus years ago. Also, I believe that after this sighting, strange things started to happen to myself that I could not explain. It was like I was looking at humans in a different way! Almost like looking through someone else's eyes at situations and people in general. Really strange and a little spooky! I am a person who has had a sighting of an object that has left me confused but also intrigued about having it, since not as many people who say they have seen a UFO are telling the truth. Some say it is science fiction but what I saw was far from that!"

The amazing thing about this case is that the theater owners were aware enough of the UFO drive-in connection that they took advantage of it and actually advertised, "Come to the drive-in and see the UFOs!"

Beyond that, this case indicates that the UFO occupants are apparently willing to put on repeat showings and encore performances at the same theater for those who might have missed the early show!

Ripon Drive-In Theater

Perhaps the most obvious feature of drive-in encounters is the tendency of UFOs to perform fantastic maneuvers well beyond the ability of conventional aircraft. Again, it's as if the UFO occupants are intentionally being dramatic, as this next case illustrates.

On April 19, 1963, four college students were at a drive-in theater near Ripon, Wisconsin when they observed a group of brightly lit circular objects traveling overhead at "tremendous" speed. Some UFOs glowed orange, while others were silvery. The objects made several non-ballistic maneuvers impossible for normal aircraft, including turning at ninety-degree angles.

Convinced that they were seeing genuine UFOs, the students phoned the police who sent an officer to investigate. Upon arrival, the police investigator himself witnessed the lights. The students later reported their sighting to UFO researchers, and their account appeared in the small UFO magazine, *Saucer News.*

Wellington Circle Twin Drive-in Theater

This next case comes from longtime pioneering researcher, Lawrence Fawcett. It's a fantastic case containing all the elements of a drive-in theater encounter: low-level objects appearing near the movie screen, performing highly dramatic maneuvers for a long period of time in front of a large group of witnesses.

One evening in May 1963, at around 9:00 p.m., movie-goers at the Wellington Circle Twin Drive-In Theater in Medford, Massachusetts were treated to a UFO display over the theater that was, as one reporter writes, "a better show than the one on the billing."

Everyone was viewing the film when their attention was drawn to strange activity in the sky above the screen. Looking up, they saw two glowing, orange-red, disc-shaped objects. Suddenly, the two discs were joined by two more, then two more after that. Finally, two more arrived until there was a grand total of eight glowing discs.

By this time, nearly everyone at the theater had exited their cars to watch the fleet of discs, which were clearly putting on a performance for them. For the next forty-five minutes, the objects moved two-by-two, splitting apart and rising up either side of the formation of discs until they reached the top. After forty-five minutes, the objects departed, leaving a very stunned group of witnesses.

The theater had twin screens with a capacity of about 900 cars. It was later doubled in size. Unfortunately, like many drive-in theaters, it didn't survive the 1970s. Now an office building stands in its place.

Southside Drive-In Theater

This next case perfectly illustrates one of the unique and prominent patterns of drive-in theater encounters: the tendency of UFOs to hover directly next to the movie screens, in a position that makes it virtually impossible for them not to be seen.

One evening in 1963, "Ashley," (age 10) her mother and two friends all decided to see the movie *Tom Jones* at the Southside Drive in at South Fort Worth, Texas. It was around 9:00 p.m., when they both saw an "oval-shaped, luminous object," rise up from behind the upper left side of the movie screen. It appeared to be hovering off in the distance. Then another rose up from behind the screen.

"They hovered there for several minutes," says Ashley. "It was one of those type of things that you cannot take your eyes off of, and you're actually speechless."

Ashley was amazed at what happened next. "The first one came, went up and a little bit to the right, although upwards, and took off so quickly. Then the other one did the same thing, both flying off together. It was almost simultaneous...it happened so quickly."

"Did you see that?" Ashley asked her mother.

"Do not say anything!" her mother replied, softly but emphatically.

Ashley could see that her mother was frightened by the object. But Ashley found it interesting and insisted on talking about it when they got home. Unfortunately, her mom made Ashley promise not to tell anyone about it.

Despite this, Ashley told her father. Strangely, their friends in the car didn't see the object, and they don't know if anyone else there saw it or not. All they know is that both of them hated the film and that the UFO sighting was "a lot more interesting than the movie."

Years after the incident, Ashley couldn't get the encounter out of her mind, and finally reported it to MUFON.

Richland Drive-In Theater

"This sighting has never left my mind," says Gordon (pseudonym.) "I will never forget what I saw."

It was 1963 (approx.,) and Gordon had taken his girlfriend to see a movie at the Richland Drive-In Theater in Johnstown, Pennsylvania. They pulled into the parking lot and found a good spot. Darkness fell upon the theater. The movie screen lit up and the pre-show began. While teasers and commercials played on the screen, the last few cars continued to trickle in.

The movie was just about to start when it happened; Gordon heard a strange "crackling sound." As the sound grew louder, Gordon and the others looked around. It was a dark night and nothing seemed to be visible.

Suddenly, the movie screen went black and the portable speakers went dead. At the same time, the cars that were still trying to enter the theater and find a spot also failed, with both headlights and car engines dying simultaneously. The crackling sound increased, but still nothing was visible.

Gordon describes what happened next: "People got out of their cars. And as we looked up, there was an object the size of a football field coming across the sky. It was shaped like a sphere, almost like a Stealth, but five times as big. There was a dome on its bottom that was illuminated and seemed to rotate. There were greenish-blue flames coming off the edges. And it went right down the skyline."

Gordon was shocked. The entire sighting lasted no more than five minutes, but it left a deep impression on him. Forty-six years after the incident, he finally decided to officially report his sighting to NUFORC.

The Richland Drive-In theater had a 450-car capacity. As of yet, no other witnesses to this event have stepped forward.

Atlanta Drive-In Theater

In many drive-in UFO encounters, the UFOs seem to have no fear of being seen. The event that occurred on June 29, 1964, at a drive-in theater in Atlanta, Georgia is a great example of a brazen UFO that appears to be posing for the witnesses. It is easily one of the most dramatic drive-in UFO encounters on record.

The main witness, Trent, (pseudonym) was only ten years old at the time of the encounter, but the events were so incredible that he will never forget them. "My father, mother, aunt and uncle and cousin went to an old drive-in movie theater outside of Atlanta," Trent explains. "This drive-in had bleachers, similar to what you would see on a small sports field. My cousin and I were watching the movie from the bleachers while our parents were still in my uncle's car, when a boy on the top row of the bleachers yelled out, 'Look, there goes a flying saucer!'

"We all looked in the direction he was looking…and there was this brightly lit white object that looked like the lid to a round candy dish, with a dome-like thing on top. This thing was moving very rapidly just above the tree-line and disappeared below the horizon."

After the object moved away, Trent stopped thinking about it and turned his attention back to the movie. Suddenly the same kid who first saw the object shouted, "Here it comes again!"

"But this time," says Trent, "the thing was coming directly toward us! Every child on those bleachers, including me and my cousin, ran for cover. We searched frantically for our parents, but could not find the car as it was quite dark, so we ran into the building that housed the projector booth and the snack bar. I told my cousin to look out and see if it was gone, and he said he didn't see it. So, we stepped back outside, and to our horror, this thing was directly overhead! We ran again, trying to find our parents in the car, and to my great relief, I heard my mom yelling, 'We are over here!' And we ran to the safety of our parents and the car."

Trent estimates that the object was about thirty feet in diameter, and now about 1000 feet high. It was dark in the center, and had slowly rotating, rectangular-shaped lights around the perimeter. After moving over the stunned theater guests for the second time, the mysterious object moved slowly toward the southeast and disappeared over some trees in the distance.

Trent turned to his father. "What was that thing?"

"I don't have the faintest idea," his father said.

Trent's father had been in the U.S. Air Force for six years. Trent was not comforted by his answer. "I was horrified by this incident," he says. "I would very much like to know if anyone else saw a UFO that looked like what we saw that night back in June 1964. As frightening as this was, I would love to see that thing again, now that I am a trained observer. If anyone could let me know what this thing was, I would sincerely appreciate it."

Trent estimates that about fifty people saw the UFO on that night. He has never seen a UFO since, and waited forty-five years before reporting his sighting to NUFORC.

Mount Shasta Drive-In Theater

A fortuitous and rare daylight drive-in UFO encounter comes from "Stacy," (age 6) who will always remember what she saw on the afternoon of June 30, 1965. Stacy's mother was driving north along Interstate 5 returning from McCloud, California to Mount Shasta. They had reached the intersection of Highway 89 when Stacy's mother suddenly pulled the car over and parked at the entrance of the Mount Shasta Drive-In theater.

Hovering directly over the drive-in theater, in full view, was, as Stacy says, "a metallic cigar-shaped object, windowless, soundless, motionless, unlighted...very low in the air, 500 [feet]. It just hung there, sort of tilted to one side. Many cars and people stopped and watched...I saw other cars stopped and people outside of them looking up into the sky. I remember my mother being awed, and all the others were watching. This cigar-shaped, metallic, windowless, soundless, unlighted object was hanging, slightly tilted, in the clear blue afternoon sky."

They observed the strange object for at least thirty minutes, until watching it almost became "boring."

"Eventually we quit watching and drove on home," says Stacy. "...it was still there when we went on, still hanging. I have always wanted to speak to others, especially those older than myself...Many, many people had to have observed this object as it was in a very visible, high traffic area, over the interchange of Highway 89 and Interstate 5 on a very, clear sunny day."

Incidentally, the Mount Shasta area is a well-known UFO hotspot.

Studio Drive-In Theater

This next case, from well-known researcher Brian Vike, involves a pregnant school-teacher and her husband, who had an encounter in August 1965 at the Studio Drive-In Theater in Culver City, California. The case is unique in that it involves what appears to be physiological effects long after the encounter occurred.

Says the teacher, "At intermission time a huge disc with lights around the edge suddenly appeared to hover above the screen. It was fairly low, but high enough that we had to bend our heads down to see it through the front windshield. My husband and I were pointing and wondering, when I looked around and saw others in cars nearby also looking and pointing. It stayed for about two minutes and then banked off for about two or three seconds before just disappearing."

The young couple was stunned. They have no idea why the UFO had hovered so closely directly over the theater. It was also curious that it appeared during the short intermission. Could this timing have been intentional?

Three months following the incident, the teacher gave birth to her daughter. That's when she noticed something else strange. Her daughter's skin would sometimes give off a weird "buzzing" sensation. It was so unusual that the witness wondered if the UFO they had seen a few months earlier was responsible and had maybe, as she says, "beamed something into my stomach."

Conway Drive-In Theater

Are UFOs putting on displays? Do the UFO occupants see all these theater-goers and use the opportunity to show off their craft? That seems to be the explanation for what happened at a drive-in in Conway, Arkansas in 1965.

Two brothers watching *Cat Ballou* noticed three lights above and to the right of the screen. The objects not only remained there for at least twenty minutes; they began to perform all kinds of non-conventional movements.

"One of them flew figure-eights around the other two," one of the brothers explains. "Suddenly two of the lights took off with great velocity and disappeared. The other light stayed in its original position."

The show wasn't over yet. "Approximately one hour later, a light came speeding back and started circling around the stationary light, then took a position next to it and stopped."

Thirty years later the witness still remembers the event vividly, and reported his sighting to NUFORC. "I finally decided to go public," he said.

Mentor Drive-In Theater

Sometimes UFO drive-in encounters are so intense that it becomes impossible to watch the movie. The encounter at a drive-in theater in Mentor, Ohio is one of the ultimate drive-in theater encounters. Cases like this one make it undeniable that ETs do have an agenda involving drive-in theaters.

It was the mid-1960s. Lewis (pseudonym) was about seven years old. He was watching the movie with his sister and their parents when his father stuck his head out the window and began staring up at the sky. Lewis's mother asked what he was looking at, and his father replied, "Look!"

Lewis remembers that his parents both looked concerned. He asked what was happening, and his father explained that there were some "funny lights" in the sky.

"I looked around," says Lewis, "and noticed that more than half of the cars around us had the adults standing outside them looking up at the lights. We all got out of the car to look. At that point, the movie was turned off. Some people were yelling for the drive-in to turn off the light so that 'they' would not see us."

For the next half-hour, the "cigar-shaped object" moved around in the sky over the theater. Little did they know that the show had only just begun. The object suddenly "came in parallel to the ground and proceeded to turn upright so it was standing on end. Then over ten shiny, disc-shaped objects shot [out] of the bottom and zoomed around in all directions and 'danced' in the sky. After about twenty minutes, they all shot back and came to a dead stop, stacking up like plates and then ascended up into the larger cigar-shaped object, which then rotated again to be parallel to the ground. And then it took off at a rapid speed and was out of sight in seconds."

After the incredible event ended, they immediately left the drive-in, and the whole family discussed the incident. Lewis's father stated his belief that the large cigar-shaped craft was a "mother ship." To this day they all remember the event, but have been unable to find any other reports of it.

Dallas Drive-In Theater

Year after year, UFOs continued to target drive-in theaters. The incredible regularity of the encounters strongly indicates an organized agenda.

At around 8:20 p.m., on September 25, 1966, Mrs. M.A. Ferraro decided to take her children to the local drive-in theater in Dallas, Texas. The movie had been playing for a short time when suddenly Ferraro noticed a "sharp blue light" just to the west of the movie screen.

Ferraro was amazed. The object was clearly not normal. "Its movements were erratic," said Ferraro, "darting downward, instantly reversing and going back west."

The light now separated into multiple objects. She watched the objects for several minutes, long enough to determine that they were not fireflies, balloons, aircraft, or anything else she could think of.

"By the time we left the movie," says Ferraro, "there were four of these lights, all in an area extending over about three degrees, all performing the exact fantastic maneuvers…they could vanish in a second, then become visible again, but far to the right, left above or below the point at which they vanished."

Ferraro had no explanation for what she was seeing and the next day decided to call the local airport. She spoke to Mr. Fetchenbach and explained what she had seen. He told her that there had been four jets with bright blue LED lights.

Ferraro is certain that the objects she saw were not jets. "Could I be wrong?" she asks. "Personally, I don't think so. Whether there were just up there or not, jets cannot streak up and down. Some went straight up or down…" She compares their speed to that of a meteor.

Getting no help from airport authorities, Ferraro eventually reported her sighting to The Civilian Research of Interplanetary

Flying Objects (CRIFO), edited by respected researcher, Leonard Stringfield, who published her account in an issue of the organization's newsletter, *Orbit.*

Southutch Drive-In Theater

For some strange reason, there are certain cases in which the UFOs decide to put on a show so spectacular that it changes people's lives. While drive-in UFO cases are dramatic by nature, a small handful, like the following, are in a league of their own.

It was the summer of 1966 (approx.,) when Pat Mitchell and his friend Mason (pseudonym), both around age 18 or 19, decided to go see the latest James Bond flick at the Southutch Drive-In Theater in their hometown of South Hutchinson, Arkansas. They found an ideal spot directly in the center of the lot.

The film began, and like all the Bond movies, this one was gripping and action-packed. Pat, who sat in the front passenger seat, was paying attention to the film when Mason suddenly shouted, "Hey, what's that?"

Pat immediately saw what Mason was looking at. Off in the distance, right above the movie screen, a bright silver object in the distance was coming right toward them. It was already low, and getting lower. As it came closer, they could see that it was a large, silver, saucer-shaped craft unlike anything they'd ever seen before.

The two young men stared with awe and fascination as the saucer leisurely approached the theater. Within a few short moments, it arrived and hovered a few hundred feet to the right side of the screen. Immediately it began to move to the left.

Now, only a few feet away from the screen itself, it proceeded to move directly behind the screen. The Southutch movie screen was one of the largest around, and measured 52 feet wide and 120 feet high. The object was so low to the ground, that the screen completely blocked their view of the saucer.

Seconds later, the object came out from behind the screen and then stopped and hovered immediately next to the left side of the screen.

The theater lot had a capacity for 625 cars. On that night, it was at least half full. Every person at the theater stared in amazement at the craft. It was impossible not to see it, as it was almost as wide as the movie screen itself.

Says Pat, "It was a typical, round, silver disc, with different colored lights going all the way around. It was really big, maybe 30-45 feet wide."

After posing for a few moments, the object moved upward about 200 feet and stopped. It remained in place for another minute, and then moved slightly upward again.

By now, the entire audience stared at the object. Some had exited their cars and were gazing upward. There was no visible panic or fear; instead everyone seemed dumbstruck. "It was glorious," Pat says, "not frightening at all. You just kind of rub your eyes. We were like, 'Oh, my God! What are we seeing?' Both our mouths just dropped, like, *what the hell is going on?*"

A few moments later, the object began to move again, heading north and circling lazily around the theater, and then heading west above West Blanchard Avenue.

"Let's follow it!" Mason shouted.

Apparently, everyone in the theater had the same idea. The James Bond movie now completely forgotten, everyone began hopping back in their cars, detaching the speakers, and screeching out of the parking lot.

Unfortunately, there was only one way out, a small two-lane road. And with Mason and Pat parked in the center of the lot, they got stuck in the stampede of cars. But they had also been among the first to leave, so only about twenty cars got out ahead of them.

Also, the object was moving slowly, perhaps twenty mph, and Mason and Pat were able to join the massive convoy of cars who chased the object down the road.

The object moved slowly enough that everyone was able to follow along. Pat stuck his head out the window, keeping his eyes on the object as it led the cars down the road.

"We followed it out probably five or six miles west of the drive-in," Pat explains. "And then it stopped again. People were pulling out into the middle of the road and stopping. People got out of their cars."

Very quickly a group of about fifty cars blocked the highway, staring at the craft. Pat and Mason remained in their car, where they had a perfect view of the saucer.

Everyone talked animatedly about the UFO. "What are we seeing?" Mason asked.

"I don't know!"

"What is it?"

Pat had never given much thought to UFOs. He'd never read about them, and knew little about them except that some people had reported them. But as the object hovered in perfect silence, randomly flashing red, yellow, blue and green lights around its perimeter -- it became clear to everyone there that they were seeing a genuine UFO.

Most amazing, the object wasn't moving away. Everyone kept exclaiming about the strangeness of what they were seeing. "Then it rose up a little bit higher," Pat says. "It was there for five or six minutes, maybe seven. And then it just shot straight up."

The object went from a dead stop to a tiny little star-like light high in the sky in about three seconds, and then it was gone. Everyone remained for a few minutes longer, talking about what they had seen, and waiting to see if the object might return. When nothing else happened, the crowd slowly broke up.

Pat and Mason headed to their homes. As far as he knows, nobody returned to the theater that night. He estimates that the entire UFO sighting lasted about fifteen minutes.

The next day, Pat was kicking himself for not bringing his camera. He had done some photography work for the local newspaper, and usually carried his camera everywhere. He and Mason scanned the newspapers, and were surprised to see that there was no story about the object. With so many witnesses, he thought for sure there would be news about the sighting.

With his own connections to the newspaper, he and Mason headed down there and talked to some of the staff. He told them of the sighting, but the staff played dumb, and said they knew nothing about it.

Pat knew that other people had called the newspaper, so that didn't make sense. Perhaps the story would come out later? But after a few more days passed with no news-story, it became clear that the newspaper wasn't going to publish a story. It was then that Pat heard rumors that some military guys had come into the newspaper office and killed the story. "They hushed it all up," Pat says, "and that's why we weren't seeing it in the paper."

Pat and his friend continued to talk about it among their friends. Some believed them, others accused them of lying or joking. Before long, talk of the event died down, and soon it was like it never happened.

Pat never heard another word about it. He eventually moved out of state. Now, decades later, he still vividly remembers seeing the UFO. He has no idea which James Bond movie was playing, which just goes to show that the sighting was far more interesting than the movie.

Pat's life changed that day. It made him a firm believer that there was something else out there. He spent many hours looking up, hoping to see another UFO. Alas, that was to be his only sighting.

Now, more than fifty years later, he still finds himself staring up at the night sky and wondering. One starlit night, his daughter caught him checking out the stars and asked him why.

He shared his story with her, and she looked at him with concern. Pat could only laugh. He knows what he saw. As he says, "I will never forget that as long as I live."

Bogalusa Drive-In Theater

In 1966, Serena (pseudonym) was eighteen-years-old. One evening in November, she arrived home from classes at Louisiana Tech University. She lived in Bogalusa, Louisiana where her parents owned a drive-in theater. Normally she would be helping them out, but it was already 9:30 p.m., and the movies were playing.

So she put on a load of laundry and decided to do a bit of night hunting. There was a little pond located about a quarter mile from the theater where she sometimes found game. She grabbed her shotgun and headlamp and headed out. She kept her headlamp off to avoid scaring away any creatures. Off in the distance, to the south, she could see the movie screen playing a film.

Serena had almost arrived at her destination, and was coming over a small rise, when she saw an amazing sight. "My attention was drawn to lights above and between the screen tower," she said. "I immediately knew it to be some kind of craft because the lights were shining pale yellow from the interior of the vehicle. The object was no more than 100 feet from the spot where I sat down. There was absolutely no sound coming from the craft."

Serena grabbed her rifle, propped it up against a small fence, and looked at the object through the riflescope. Magnified four times, she could now see the strange craft in detail. "The upper dome of the craft had a row of six or seven trapezoid-shaped windows on the forward side," she said. "And I could see a large set of panel instruments to the rear. There were six occupants inside, three at the panels and three milling around in front of the windows intermittently watching the movie. They were all men, wearing jumpsuits which appeared green, but with the yellow interior lights I could not be certain. I observed them moving around inside the cabin of the craft, and often one or the other from the rear of the craft would walk forward to look at some part of the movie. At that time, they were right in front of the windows."

The craft was unlike anything she had ever seen. It hovered perfectly silent and still. The windows were large, at least two feet high. The occupants inside looked like human beings. It appeared that they were just leisurely watching the movie.

Serena decided she was observing a military test craft piloted by U.S. Air Force personnel. "They were clearly our military people," she says.

Her own father was in the Air Force and used to tell all kinds of stories about how he and his fellow officers would play jokes on each other. After about fifteen minutes of observing the men in the craft, Serena decided to "mess with them" and let them know that they were being observed.

"I thought the guys inside the craft would appreciate my joke," she says. "I stood up and shined my headlamp directly into the windows of the craft."

The results of Serena's joke were dramatic and instantaneous. The yellow lights inside the craft immediately flashed to red. At the same time, a loud whining noise emanated from the craft. It was a familiar sound. Her parents owned a DC generator for the theater, and it sounded exactly like it.

The whining increased to a stable frequency, at which point the object moved slowly off toward the north and then started looping west. At this point, red and green navigation lights switched on, along with a white strobe-light.

Serena knew that her dad was probably in the ticket office, which was about 300 yards away. She had been running marathons in school. She could make it there in moments. She took off running.

When she arrived at the ticket office, her surprised dad looked at her like she was crazy. Serena quickly pointed out the strange object in the sky. "He and I watched for about thirty seconds as the object crossed the sky, back lit by the lights of the paper mill to the south," Serena says.

She turned to her father. "What do you think that was?"

"An airplane," he replied.

Serena shook her head. "It was stationary in the sky," she told him. "I watched it for fifteen minutes. There were Air Force-type guys inside watching the movie."

"Uh-huh," her father said, obviously skeptical and concerned.

Serena started to explain further, at which point her father made it clear that he didn't believe her and began to question if she was on drugs or something.

Serena decided to keep quiet. She didn't talk about it for fifty-three years. In 2019, at age seventy-one, she finally decided to report her sighting to MUFON. "I no longer care if people question my sanity," she says.

Highland Drive-In Theater

A curious after-effect of a UFO encounter is that sometimes witnesses do not discuss what they just saw. This strange lack of conversation about an obviously bizarre experience turns up in several drive-in theater cases, including the following.

This next case of UFOs showing off to a crowd of theater-goers occurred at the Highland Drive-In Theater in Salt Lake City, Utah. One evening around dusk in July 1967, "Alex," (age 7) his sister and their parents entered the drive-in. Looking up they saw a "silver, metallic, disc-shaped craft" hovering about a quarter mile away to the east.

"It made no sound, and didn't have any lights," said Alex. "It just hovered in the air, then it headed north along the face of the mountains at an incredible speed. It was out of sight in a second. Then it reversed its course and came back along the same path, heading south along the face of the mountains until it was out of sight...Other people at the drive-in also saw it. Everyone looked but no one said anything, or really seemed to react to what they saw. Once it was gone, no one said anything [and] just continued as if nothing had happened. Shock perhaps?"

Following the sighting, Alex learned that other people in town, including his older sister at home, also saw the object. Two days later, an article appeared in the local paper detailing the incident.

Duluth Drive-In Theater

One case investigated by Project Blue Book occurred on May 20, 1968 at a drive-in theater in Duluth, Minnesota. The main witness was U.S. Army Lt. Robert T. Rogers, Director of Air Defense Artillery, 29 Air Division.

Rogers was at the theater with many others when a glowing white, convex lens-shaped object appeared. It blinked off and on at irregular intervals as it moved overhead about forty-five degrees above the horizon-line. It first moved northwest using smooth, but erratic maneuvers, then turned toward the west. It was visible for about five minutes before finally moving out of sight.

There was a cloudy overcast of about 5500 feet, so the object was at least that low.

Rogers called the local Duluth Airport who forwarded him to Project Blue Book. USAF Lt. William B. Stoecker interviewed Rogers, prepared a report and forwarded it to Wright Patterson Air Force Base. The case was also provided to the University of Colorado for the Condon Committee who had been contracted by the Air Force to study UFOs.

Stoecker was impressed by Rogers' testimony and wrote in his report, "The observer is known by this officer and is reliable. The light did not resemble aircraft. Balloons do not go against the wind. Satellites do not fly under clouds, and meteors do not stay in the sky for minutes or change course. Ball lightning is unlikely according to weather officer. Sighting: unexplained."

Despite Stoecker's conclusions, Blue Book superiors declined to include the case in their list of unsolved cases, and requested further investigation into the possibility that the object was a balloon.

Longview Drive-In Theater

Not all drive-in theater encounters are obvious displays meant to be seen by everyone. In this next case, a UFO appeared directly over a drive-in, but was observed by only a single witness.

One evening in July 1969, a family of four went to the drive-in theater in Longview, Texas. The mother, "Anne," noticed that it was a clear night with lots of stars. The movie was boring, so she was looking up at the stars when suddenly they became blotted out by a large, dark object.

"I saw this huge triangular-shaped craft going slowly from west to east," said Anne. "It had no sound and moved about the speed of a small private airplane...It appeared to be fairly flat on the bottom, and I couldn't see any depth due to the fact that I was very close to being under it...I was in awe of what I was looking at."

Anne screamed for her husband to look, but by then, it had already passed by. Nobody else at the theater seemed to notice the object. To this day, she wonders if it was an advanced military craft, or extraterrestrial.

Foothill Drive-In Theater

One month later, on August 12, 1969, UFOs visited a drive-in theater in Azusa, California. Again, despite the fact that the parking lot was filled with cars, apparently only two people observed the object.

It was her sixteenth birthday, and "Susanne" and her family decided to celebrate by going to the Foothill Drive-In to watch a double feature of *How the West Was Won* and *The War Wagon.* The intermission came and they had just purchased some more snacks when Susanne's mother screamed, "What is that?"

She pointed upward at a "typical saucer-shaped metallic craft with rotating lights." The object was above the drive-in screen, but south of their position, moving at a slow pace. Then suddenly it banked to the side and took off upward.

"The speed of acceleration was so incredibly fast," says Susanne. "No known airplane or jet could accelerate that fast. It was the blink of an eye. We looked out of the car to see if anyone within our sight was pointing toward the sky, but we couldn't see anyone behind us."

Although there were about fifty cars there, nobody else seemed to see it. Says Susanne, "My mother would not talk about it afterward. She seemed visibly shaken. I will never forget it. It changed my life."

Although now closed, for many years it was the last operating drive-in west of Oklahoma along the famed Route 66.

Kings Drive-In Theater

In some cases, drive-in theater encounters appear to be part of a complex of local sightings.

It was 4:30 p.m., on August 20, 1970, and Larry Wilson and his friend Charles Hill (both teen-agers at Lemoore High School), were driving through the town of Lemoore, California. Suddenly they saw a saucer-shaped craft, navy gray in color, hovering about 1500 feet above *Cal-King Livestock Yards.* As the object began to move north, they decided to chase it.

The boys followed the object for about four minutes, and were able to get a clear view of the object as it zipped off at high speed. Both witnesses noticed a thin gray contrail being emitted from the craft.

Both boys were amazed by what they had seen and assumed that the encounter was over. But later that evening, Larry Wilson and another friend, decided to go see a movie at the Kings Drive-In Theater.

It was around 11:00 p.m., when his friend, Roger Graham, who also attended the drive-in movie in his own car, called out to Larry to look at the strange object in the sky. Both boys looked up and observed a silver disc that was shaped similar to the craft he had seen earlier that day. They watched it for about three minutes as it moved slowly north toward the city of Laton, disappearing off in the distance.

Southside Drive-In Theater

Most drive-in theater encounters are observed by the entire audience. This next case is a good example of a sighting witnessed by hundreds of people.

It was around 1970 and "Andrew" was about thirteen years old when he went with his sister, brothers and parents to the Southside Drive-in Theater in Youngstown, Ohio. While watching the movie, Andrew's attention was drawn away from the screen by the sight of the people in front of them exiting their cars, looking and pointing at something in the sky. Andrew and his parents jumped out of their vehicle, and saw an amazing sight. A few miles away, a large glowing object was "darting all over the place, up, down, left and right, back and forth."

After darting around, it dropped down behind some trees and rose up seconds later from a different area. For the next five minutes, the object danced around in the same manner "much faster than any plane or helicopter."

Finally, it darted away. Everyone at the drive-in had been watching with breathless silence. Now a huge chatter broke out and everyone began to discuss what they had just seen. All the theater-goers were asking what the object was.

Says Andrew, "I asked Dad, 'What was that?' Laughingly, Dad said, 'A UFO.' We never talked about that night after that, I don't know why."

Almost fifty years later, Andrew still remembers the incident. He estimates that there were about 200 people who observed the object.

Paramount Drive-In Theater

While some of the drive-in sightings do seem to be a matter of luck, cases like this next one are outright displays.

This classic case of a drive-in targeted by UFOs occurred in 1972 in Paramount, California. At the time, Claudia Blacios was only five years old when her parents took her and her sister to a drive-in movie. They piled into the family's Volkswagen Beetle and headed off to their location. The parking lot was filled with people. It had just started getting dark. The movie started.

Without warning, a strange metallic-silver object appeared immediately adjacent to and above the movie screen. "They had turned on the film," Claudia says. "My sister and I were messing around in the back. All of a sudden, we see people running past us, and cars honking, and headlights turning on and off. I don't know what's going on. I hear a lady screaming."

Claudia turned to her dad. "What's going on?" she asked.

"Nothing," he replied.

Claudia was not convinced. "So, I looked between the seats to look at my mom and dad to see why they were acting so weird, and why all those people were walking so fast to their cars and dropping their popcorn. I saw my dad's face, and it was just completely frozen and just pale. And my mom's was too.

"And all of a sudden, I look out the window and I see a strange thing. It wasn't a plane...it was kind of like a cigar...It was metallic."

"Look!" she told her sister. "Look!"

"We're just staring at this thing, and people are fighting to go out the exits that are in the front and the back. Cars are honking and a lot of people are leaving. And my dad just sat there and didn't do anything. I was just looking at it."

The object was shiny silver "like a spoon." It had strangely-shaped portholes around the circumference, a bright light on the bottom, and was making a strange whirring sound. "Like a droning sound," Claudia explains, "but it was very faint in-between all the screaming."

"It was there for a while," she says. "It was kind of like watching us watch the movie. And I thought that was really odd, because why would it want to watch what we're watching?...and then eventually it went straight up."

As in other cases, Claudia and her family didn't discuss the incident afterward. "I remember my mom and dad never talked about it again. It was just one of those things you don't ever think about."

Many years later, as an adult, Claudia (now an office clerk) was listening to the radio when the subject turned to UFOs. People began to call-in and share their encounters. A gentleman came on the line and began to talk about his close-up encounter with a metallic disc at a drive-in theater in Paramount, California. He then proceeded to describe exactly what she had seen back in 1972.

Claudia was shocked. "He was at the same drive-in theater at the same time," she says, "watching the same movie, and described the same thing."

Claudia's mom was also listening. Claudia turned to her and said, "We were there!"

"Yeah," her mom replied. "That was a long time ago."

"Why didn't we ever talk about it?"

"I don't know."

Claudia was amazed. "That guy was describing the events just as I remember them, with the ship being there, and people leaving."

The Paramount theater is still in operation today.

Kam Drive-In Theater

The behavior of UFOs over drive-in theaters makes it clear that the UFO occupants have little fear of being observed.

One dramatic encounter took place one year after the above incident at the Kam Drive-in Theater in Honolulu, Hawaii.

One night in June 1973, a married couple was watching "some cheesy movie" when they became distracted by something much more interesting.

"Something caught my eye," says the husband, "and I thought that someone threw a frisbee or pizza box over our car. I took a direct look at it, and it was something else entirely! It was a large UFO...headed toward the sea, but it was only 200 feet above, and about 75-90 feet wide...You could see the shape due to the reflection of the city lights on the bottom of it."

The object was totally silent. It moved directly over the movie screen. "Then," says the witness, "other people in the drive-in who saw it started honking their car horns!"

The object didn't vary in its path and didn't seem to react to the honking horns. Instead, it continued over and behind the screen, moving slowly out of view.

Winnipeg Drive-In Theater

This next case is a typical example of a first-class drive-in UFO encounter: an object hovering at extremely low elevation right next to the movie screen.

It was the evening of July 7, 1973, and "Chuck" (age 20) and his girlfriend were attending the Winnipeg Drive-In Theater at the corner of King Edward and Ellice Avenue in Winnipeg, Manitoba in Canada. The area of the drive-in was in the middle of town. The local airport was about one-quarter mile away from the theater. It had just gotten dark, and the movie was about to begin. That's when Chuck and his girlfriend noticed a brass-colored object hovering about 100 feet directly above the movie screen.

"Do you see what I see?" his girlfriend asked.

"Yes," Chuck replied.

Chuck could hardly believe his eyes. "I got out of my car as it made its move away and it simply vanished, or better yet, blended in with the darkness...it slowly moved away, and with its brassy coloring, simply disappeared into the darkness."

The next day, Chuck reported his sighting and was told that what he had seen was the *Champs Chicken* advertising balloon.

Chuck disagreed, as the object was far too low and close to the screen to be an advertising balloon.

"Why did they lie to me?" Chuck asks. "I know now that it was real. There were probably at least another seventy-five cars there, and we all must have seen it."

Fort Lauderdale Drive-In Theater

As we have seen, in some cases the military appears and chases the UFO away. This next case provides a disturbing example. It comes from "Bradley," (pseudonym) and his girlfriend, who were attending a drive-in theater in Fort Lauderdale, Florida in 1973.

At some point during the movie, the management of the theater interrupted the movie and announced that a UFO was flying over the theater, that it was not a hoax, but an actual UFO.

Bradley and the other theater-goers were amazed to see the object performing a dramatic display overhead. "The object was large and disc-shaped," Bradley says. "It was like two plates on top of each other, with a top that looked like a Reese's [peanut-butter cup] turned upside down. It had windows which were lit up, and there were beings looking out the craft. It was about 50-60 feet in the air."

Bradley stared at the object in awe, while his girlfriend was too frightened to look. She put her head in her lap and began crying in fear.

Bradley felt no fear. "Look," he told her. "This is a chance of a lifetime. We might never get another one!"

She refused to look. Bradley's eyes remained glued to the object as it maneuvered around the theater. "It moved slowly over the place," he said. "It turned around very slowly as it went from east to west. Then it went over the airport tower and hovered. Then it turned into a white ball of light, and a small red light came out of it and flew around very fast. The object then flew straight up and out of sight."

The drama wasn't over yet. At some point police and government officials showed up and evacuated the theater. "We were told to leave in a single file," Bradley says. "As we left, the military told everyone not to speak about this to anyone."

Baltimore Drive-In Theater

If drive-in UFO cases tell us anything, it's that these locations are, at the very least, ideal places to see a UFO. It was after midnight one March evening in 1974, and "Ellen" was driving home from work. On the radio, there was talk about a possible meteor sighting over the area. She didn't give it much thought, but continued toward her home in Baltimore, Maryland.

Then strange things began to happen. First her car went through the overpass and mysteriously stalled for "just a split second." Then, as she approached her home, she saw "a formation of orange lights in the distance ahead, over the treetops. She first thought they were station tower lights, but realizing they were strange, she changed her route and headed toward them. They now appeared to be about a mile away, but as she drove forward, she realized they were much closer. Suddenly they were almost directly overhead, hovering alongside the road.

"They now appeared to be hovering over a freshly plowed field at 500-1000 feet altitude," said Ellen. "[It] was a trapezoidal configuration with two objects in the front and two others following slightly farther apart in the rear."

Realizing she was seeing an actual UFO, Ellen didn't hesitate. "I panicked and made a sharp right turn at the intersection, under the objects, and floored my car down the road. As I fled the scene, I looked over my shoulder to the left, or in the rear-view mirror, and I distinctly saw the four objects had come closer together and were descending toward the ground. That was the last I saw of them, but it is not the end of the story."

Ellen rushed home and told her father and brother what she had seen. They were skeptical, and her brother said that she probably saw helicopters. It wasn't long, however, before Ellen received confirmation of her sighting.

"The very next day," Ellen says, "I was standing in line at the local fast-food restaurant, and I saw a girl there. So, I asked her if she had seen anything unusual the night before. Her eyes bugged out."

"Did you see those four orange lights too?" her friend asked.

Ellen told her that she did see the lights. "And she told me that she and her friends had been at the local drive-in movie theater nearby when the lights passed overhead."

Ellen's friend told her, "Everybody stopped watching the movie and got out of their cars to look at what they were."

Ellen was shocked, but also pleased. "At least I had some validation of my sighting," she says.

She later returned to where she had seen the UFO lowering down to the ground to look for landing traces, but was unable to locate anything unusual.

Hinesville Drive-In Theater

Almost without exception, drive-in theater encounters can be classified as a sighting. Most fall under the Hynek classification system as a close encounter of the first kind. Some, however, do affect the environment, and would be classified as a close encounter of the second kind. This next case, involving an apparent observed abduction, is perhaps unique among drive-in UFO cases, and involves an apparent close encounter of the third kind.

In April 1974, Derek Smith (a U.S. Army Ranger) and his wife decided to attend a drive-in movie in Hinesville, Georgia. Going to the drive-in was a fun weekend activity which they enjoyed on a regular basis. On this particular evening, the real show would take place off-screen, in the skies above.

"I don't even remember what the movie was," says Smith, "but I noticed a bright light in the sky about three or four times the size of Venus. It was a very clear night and this bright light seemed to be moving slowly downward and eventually went behind the movie screen."

"Are you looking at that light too?" his wife asked.

"Yes," he said.

"I've been watching it," his wife replied, "and it doesn't seem right."

The light was disc-shaped. At first it was high in the sky, but then it descended to about 300-400 feet. It emerged from behind the screen and began to flash from white to red to orange and then yellow. Then it turned bright purple and maneuvered up, sideways, down and sideways again, tracing a square-pattern in the sky.

The object then remained still, and sent down a beam of light to the ground.

"That is neat!" Smith told his wife, "shooting down a beam of light like that!"

Then the beam of light did something it shouldn't be able to do: the beam stopped coming from the craft, but remained visible and continued to descend to the ground until it disappeared. The light beam itself was detached from the disc.

Immediately, a white beam of light shot up from the ground and hit the disc. Then something happened which stunned Smith and his wife.

"While my wife and I were watching the beam go up to the craft," says Smith, "We saw something inside the beam that reminded me of a person, with arms and legs spread-eagled, tumbling and turning slowly inside that light beam...there was something floating upward in the beam of light. My first impression was that it was a person because I could see four long appendages, like arms and legs, and one short appendage, like a head...then the object just stayed there, hovering, motionless and silent."

Afterward, another disc approached and seemed to physically merge with the first one. "A few minutes later," says Smith, "the large object descended to almost treetop level and slowly meandered off to the northeast until it was out of our view."

Smith and his wife left the theater and drove around to try and get a closer look, but the object was gone. Did they observe somebody being abducted by a UFO? Could it have been an ET? Did anyone else see it? Smith and his wife are unsure. Smith, himself, has had several other close-up encounters.

East Park Drive-In Theater

Many UFOs that hover over drive-ins perform incredible maneuvers in an apparent attempt to draw the attention of the audience. Sometimes, they resort to even stronger methods, as this next excellent case shows.

It was early June in 1974. Dee and five of her friends had recently graduated from high school and decided to begin their summer vacation by viewing a midnight showing of the movie, *The Exorcist*, at the East Park Drive-In Theater in Syracuse, New York. When they arrived at the theater, the earlier "sunset" crowd was still vacating the premises. Finally, all the other cars left, and to their surprise, Dee and her friends discovered that they were the only car watching the midnight showing.

They were about half-way through the movie when their attention became distracted by strange lights flashing on the screen.

At first, they assumed the projectionist was messing around. Then they noticed that the area around their car had become strangely illuminated, as if a searchlight was shining down on them from above.

One of the friends stuck his head out the window and looking up, shouted, "Good God!"

Instantly, the teen-agers threw open the car doors, jumped out of the car and looked up.

"Above us was a bright disc-shaped object," Dee says. "It was perhaps the width of four or five car parking slots, and it was hovering over our car. The disc-shaped object glowed and had lights evenly spaced around its outer edge."

To their amazement, the disc appeared to be flashing lights directly at the screen while the movie was playing. "We wondered if they were trying to communicate with the people in the movie or something," Dee said. "Then the disc, whatever it was, just shot off into the night sky. We threw the drive-in speaker out of the car window and drove off in a hurry."

A few miles down the road, they came upon a police officer in his cruiser. They got out to report their sighting and discovered a small group of other people from the area who were also telling the officer about the UFO that they had just witnessed. The officer seemed skeptical and was more interested in calming the people down than in recording the facts of their encounters.

Dee says that the sighting left her deeply shaken. More than forty years later, she still remembers it vividly.

Ascot Park Drive-In Theater

This next incredible (and somewhat concerning) case comes from Scott J. Santa, who answered my social media request for drive-in theater encounters. It took place in Cuyahoga Falls, Ohio, thirty-five miles south of Cleveland. It is, perhaps, the ultimate drive-in UFO encounter. What follows is Santa's own written account of his experience at the Ascot Park Drive-In Theater, now known as the Ascot Triple Drive-In, (capacity: 400 cars.)

"In August 1974 [date approx.,] a friend of mine, Mike, [pseudonym] and I had nothing going on and decided to go to the drive-in movies. It was a beautiful summer evening -- not a cloud in the sky -- stars everywhere. We paid for our tickets, drove in and parked in the back, of course, hoping to find a car full of ladies. Not quite a full house but there was a gang of kids playing at the playground just under and in front of the screen. Everyone was settled in and ready to watch a couple of movies. A normal and mundane a night if ever there was one.

"As we got some food and drinks and started to watch the cartoons, I could just make out something approaching the screen from behind and above. And just like that, a huge -- and I do mean HUGE -- chevron came into view over the top and above the screen. It dwarfed the parking area.

"I asked Mike if he could see it.

"'Yes, what the hell is that?' was the reply.

"Its speed of advance was incredibly slow," Scott Santa says, "best guess is approximately 10-15 mph. It seemed to float rather than fly. It had no lights. It was so black, it blotted out the stars in the sky, and was utterly silent. Mike and I each got out of the car and stared at this thing. Again, the size of this craft (for want of a better term) was enormous. From wing to wing, it overlapped the drive-in enclosure. In fact, it dwarfed it. The proverbial, 3-4 football fields. It proceeded in a straight line right over the top of the first row of cars. By now I could see that almost everyone was out of their vehicles and pointing and looking around, quite possibly to make sure everyone else was seeing the same thing.

"As it continued on -- not quite immediately over my head -- *all* of the lights in the drive-in went out. The movie stopped, the concession stand went black. I noticed that several people were trying to start their cars and leave. None of the cars would start. As difficult as this is to explain -- I was aware of all of that -- but my recollection is that I really never took my eyes off of the object. There wasn't any panic, but I could tell some of the folks were completely terrified, yet zombified if you will.

"Mike and I weren't speaking by this time. At this juncture I felt as if I was the only one there, (though I wasn't,) so my eyes and extreme focus was staring at this thing as it continued on its way. By the time it made it right over top of us, I could feel that something wasn't quite right. I could see and actually feel that the air around us was shimmering as it were, like you see on top of asphalt or cement on a hot day. The air 'felt' heavy and we both felt that it was difficult to move. My ears popped even though it was completely silent around us. I could hear Mike, but we could not hear anything else, like any of the other people talking or yelling... nothing. The shimmering air had the effect of making one feel as if you were walking underwater, if you will...now known as the 'OZ effect.' I felt that if I could have reached down and picked up a larger piece of the gravel, I could have thrown it and hit this thing -- that's how close it appeared.

"I was struck again by the complete and utter silence around us. Everyone seemed to be in a funk and just standing around looking at this thing. It never veered or changed direction and hovered over top of the park for what seemed like ten minutes, though I cannot be sure of the length of time. It was traveling from the west and proceeding in an easterly direction. When it cleared the vacant property, a vast field of undeveloped real estate behind the drive-in, the 'OZ effect' disappeared and you could feel as if a weight had been lifted off of you. *All* of the lights flicked back on, and the movie started again. Just like that -- like a switch had been flipped.

"I continued to watch this object until it disappeared from my view in the distance. It never changed course and 'flew' or floated in a straight line. It was incredible. Once I lost sight of it, I got back in my car, almost robotic-like, and completely forgot all about what I just witnessed. Mike and I did not speak to each other about it ever -- we just carried on with the movie as if nothing happened. At least, this is my recollection. Apparently, so did everyone else in the park. No one, I mean *nobody*, was running around asking questions or doing anything but watching the movie.

"I recall having to go to the bathroom sometime afterwards and as usual, there was a bit of a line to get in. No one talked about it, no one said a word about what just happened. When the movie was over, I don't remember leaving or what happened afterwards. That is a complete blank. But obviously I dropped Mike off and went home, completely forgetting what just happened.

"I have no idea what time I got home that night or even what time we left, another complete blank. I never told my brother, or my parents. In fact, I have a bit of a black hole in my memory from that point on until some years later. I was in a bookstore and happened upon a paperback edition of Edward Ruppelt's [book], *The Report on Unidentified Flying Objects*, and BANG! the experience flooded upon me as if a gate had been opened.

"I had to sit down and absorb it as I was almost overwhelmed by it. I had lost contact with Mike by then, and was unable to verify with him. But in my mind's eye, it's as clear as the day is long. I have my suspicions about 'missing time,' and after years of reflection that possibly something other than a CE sighting happened, but have never explored that aspect. In fact, I highly suspect that something else may have happened to me personally, maybe everyone else in the park as well, I do not know, I cannot recall, but there is that gut instinct that continuously nags at me that there was something, some further interaction, something I was supposed to do. That is the itch that has never gone away.

"I was, without question confronted with *something* that was distinctly impossible, but it happened as I described, despite the fantastic scenario that was manifested.

"I now no longer have the luxury of disbelief. It has been suggested to me to put an ad in the local paper to see if there was anyone else that had happened to recall that. After mulling that option over, I decided it would not be such a great idea. I can only imagine the responses I may get. But I'm okay with that at this point. Like I stated previously, I now no longer have the luxury of disbelief, nor do I need validation from anyone. Like the James Fox movie, *I Know What I Saw*. I just don't know what it did to me...if anything. A most confusing event that I wish I had an explanation for."

Santa's case was first presented in Ryan Sprague's excellent book, *Somewhere in the Skies*. Sprague was impressed by the case. As he writes, "Scott's account is compelling to say the least. Here was a case in which many people witnessed a massive object floating overhead. And yet, after its disappearance, no one spoke of it. One would assume that mass panic would have ensued, and that everyone would have caused a frenzy. Yet something kept everyone there, motionless. Why did Scott believe that he and others reacted this way?"

Sprague asked Santa this question. Santa replied, "I do not recall the incident with any fear whatsoever. I do have a feeling of something awe-inspiring, but not fear inducing at all...It was definitely a positive awe-inspiring encounter. But having that time gap is a disturbing issue, as well as my non-action or immediate shutdown on recall."

Sprague was particularly struck by the brazen behavior of the object. He writes, "One of the most intriguing things about Scott's sighting was how blatant the craft was in terms of being seen both to himself and everyone at the drive-in that night. I wanted to know if he thought that this was all by chance."

Scott Santa told Sprague, "I believe I just happened to be in the right place at the right time, or we possibly could have been a target of opportunity."

The theater was closed in 1984, and has now been replaced with residential housing.

Portland Twin Drive-In Theater

In some cases, when a UFO hovers over a drive-in, people react by honking their horns or flashing their lights. Sometimes, however, the UFOs come too close for comfort, and people react with complete panic, such as what happened on June 15, 1975 at the Portland Twin Drive-in Theater in Scarborough, Maine.

James [pseudonym] and another witness were driving into the theater when he first noticed a strange object to the southeast, glowing a yellow-orange from underneath. "I didn't think too much about it," James said, "but I kept looking that way, and it was still there."

Even after they drove in and parked, the object remained. A half-hour later, James saw that the object had moved. It was cruising about 50-75 feet altitude over the town of Scarborough and was heading directly toward them. "I thought it was strange," says James, "so I kept looking over at it."

He estimates the object was about a mile away when it moved slowly closer until it was hovering over the shopping center next door. James watched as people at the shopping center began to drop their bags and run away. It was so close that he was able to see that the object was white on top and had panels around the bottom with square-lights flashing a yellow-orange strobing light.

The object slowly moved toward them. It took about ten minutes, and now it moved directly overhead. "I could have hit it with a rock," James says.

Everyone at the theater observed the object move first behind the screen, turn to the east, come back over the screen and hover about fifteen feet above it. "By this time," says James, "people were going nuts. Women were screaming. Cars [were] tearing speakers off. It was just crazy."

The object wasn't done yet. After practically clearing out the theater where James was parked, the object now moved over to another screen and did the same thing. "It was about 20-25 feet in diameter," says James. "it was just hovering there for at least five minutes."

By the time it was gone, most of the people in the drive-in had fled in terror. Says James, "Ten to fifteen cars stayed after it left. Some of us stayed and talked. Now, I am a big chicken, but I wasn't afraid. I think I was in shock. It did not hit me until I got home."

James waited forty years before reporting his sighting to NUFORC. As he says, "To this day, if I tell someone the whole story, by the end I am shaking." He is still looking for anyone else who may have been there.

Belleville Drive-In Theater

In several cases, drive-in UFO encounters are so dramatic that they make it impossible to watch the movie. In this next case, the display was so fantastic, it not only stopped the movie, it attracted the attention of the local military.

The encounter occurred in Belleville, Illinois in October 1975. "My wife and I were at a drive-in theater around Belleville, near Scott AFB," writes Nathan (pseudonym.) "The movie was *Last Tango in Paris*. About a half hour into the movie, one or more objects started dashing back and forth across the sky and [with] high velocity and seemingly high altitude."

When the activity continued, all the theater-goers began to pay more attention to the objects than to the movie itself. Says Nathan, "Eventually they turned off the screen so everyone could see better. At least a hundred people saw this. Everyone got out of their cars to watch."

Unfortunately, the display was put to a sudden end. "Soon several jets appeared and chased them off to the west," Nathan says. "I've often thought of this over the years, but have never seen any press on it."

Mile High Drive-In Theater

While this next case is fairly typical, it exhibits the now familiar attributes of a drive-in encounter, and it provides further evidence of the ETs' agenda to regularly show themselves to small groups of people at drive-in theaters.

One evening sometime in 1975, a lady was at the Mile High Drive-In Theater in Denver, Colorado to watch *Dr. Zhivago*. More than 100 people were there when a large circular disc with lights around the perimeter showed up, apparently to investigate.

As explained by the witness's husband: "Everyone there saw a huge flying saucer rising up behind and somewhat to the left of the screen. Everyone got out of their cars and watched as this thing slowly rose then came to a complete standstill, hovering."

The object remained for only a few moments, then tilted at a forty-five-degree angle and accelerated out of view, leaving everyone astounded.

Riverside Drive-In Theater

One of several people who answered my request for cases is "Joseph." He's unsure of the date, sometime in the 1970s, but he remembers that it took place directly across from the Lee Lanes Bowling Alley, at the Riverside Drive-In Theater, in Vandergrift, Pennsylvania.

Says Joseph, "Me and my wife were sitting at the drive-in. Behind the screen, there was this tall hillside approximately 100 feet high. Out of the corner of my eye, I spotted something moving across the sky, fairly bright. It would move left, then right, then up, then down. Then all of a sudden it shot straight up and out of sight."

Joseph is convinced it was a genuine UFO. As he says, "It wasn't a plane, that's for sure!"

Boulder Drive-In Theater

A wonderfully dramatic example of a UFO attracted to a drive-in occurred in July 1976 at an outdoor theater in Boulder, Colorado. It's one of few cases in which the UFO seemed to react to the audience.

Kedrick (pseudonym) was with his girlfriend at the drive-in when she shouted out, "What's that?"

"At the same time," Kedrick explains, "I noticed a lighted craft approaching from the southwest. At first it appeared to be a helicopter flying low and making slow gradual turns back and forth. As it got closer, I could see that the lighting and motions were definitely not standard for a helicopter, or any other aircraft. The object seemed to be attracted by the movie playing on the screen, and approached and hovered over the cars parked at the theater."

Kedrick estimates that the object was only about 200 feet overhead. It was a "classic domed saucer," he said, with red, orange and yellow lights flashing slowly. The disc then began to descend even lower; at the same time, the lights became brighter and began to flash more quickly. Suddenly the disc began to extend a "rectangular structure" from the bottom, which flashed extremely bright green, blue and purple lights.

Says Kedrick, "The intensity of the lights became almost painful to look at. The other people at the drive-in reacted by honking their horns and flashing their headlights, at which point, the object moved away."

Yuma Drive-In Theater

In most sightings, UFOs are seen for only a few moments and quickly race away or disappear. However, drive-in UFO encounters have the unique feature of sometimes lasting for a long time. As reported by Roger Marsh, (MUFON Director of Communications and the editor of the MUFON UFO Journal) in September 1976, an extended family of four was attending a drive-in movie theater in Yuma, Arizona, when something very strange happened.

Kathy (pseudonym) was there with her young daughter, stepbrother and mother. She was watching the movie when her attention became distracted by a row of dim lights off in the distance. At first, she assumed that it was just a plane, but when she looked again, the object was still there.

"After about 20 to 30 minutes of glancing at what I assumed were window lights," says Kathy, "I realized this 'plane' was not moving, nor was it making any sound, and realized it was not a plane. I stood up on the bed of the truck and told those with me to look."

The object was still dim and off in the distance, so Kathy had to point it out for the others to see it. But at that moment, it began to move closer. The object was still dark and hard to see, but it kept approaching until it was directly over the truck. Only then did everyone see that it was a classic saucer-shaped object with little lights or portholes around the circumference. "At that moment," Kathy says, "it began moving, wobbling and began going upward, with its shape changing into a typical saucer shape."

"I see it!" Kathy's stepbrother shouted. "Look!"

"At that time," Kathy says, "it began flopping from one side to the other several times. With each flop it got smaller, like it was moving away. We were both trying to get my mother to see it, and she did at the point just before it went away. It was gone in a breath, but left twinkly sparkles behind it."

Twin Drive-In Theater

If the ETs' agenda of targeting drive-in theaters is to impress the witnesses and convince them of the reality of UFOs, then this agenda has been remarkably successful. Most witnesses who report these kinds of sightings, such as the following, remember their encounters in vivid detail, and are convinced that they saw something extremely unusual.

It was June 10, 1977, and "Andrew," his wife, daughter and niece were attending the Twin Drive-In Theater in Stockton, California to enjoy a showing of the new blockbuster movie, *King Kong*. It was dusk as the screens came to life and began the advertisements before the movie. That's when Andrew noticed an unusual-looking aircraft approaching from the west.

"At first I thought it was just a small airplane," Andrew said. "I noticed some lights, but they were not compatible with any aircraft I had seen."

At the time, Andrew worked at the local Stockton Airport and was used to seeing aircraft, so when he couldn't identify what he was seeing, he became intrigued.

"My interest turned from the movie I really wanted to see, to something in the sky," he says. "I became totally involved watching this craft which skirted the sky over downtown Stockton. I remember saying, 'I bet the guys in the airport tower are looking at this thing."

By this point, the movie had begun. Andrew alerted his family to the strange object, but they were already absorbed by the movie. Andrew, however, kept his eye glued to the apparent UFO. "I kept watching from my car while the movie proceeded. This craft, after a while, seemed to be coming back our way. I got out of the car when I realized it was coming directly over us. I was scared because at some point during this event, I knew what I was seeing was something I had not seen before -- a totally silent craft, extremely slow moving, with confusing lights.

"I watched it come directly over us, maybe 200 feet or less. This was not some streak of light or a blur you might have problems seeing. It passed right over our heads, a saucer-shaped craft, maybe fifty feet in diameter. It seemed to consist of two sections, or if not, had rotating lights that flashed as it revolved gave that impression. They were bright white and went alternately off and on as the craft revolved. I just stood there in awe as it passed silently overhead. My wife and the kids witnessed it."

Andrew was stunned. The entire incident left him shaken. "I thought the next day the local paper would have some unusual headlines. Not a word. Not a word from any news source. No one at the airport tower mentioned it. No one at the drive-in got out of their car as I did. What did we see? A U.S. top secret aircraft flying over downtown Stockton? This was not the Nevada desert. Whoever controlled this craft cared not who saw it. Which brings up the most perplexing question to me: did anyone else see it at all? And how could they not?"

Many years later, Andrew is still searching for answers. "I'm sixty years old now," he says. "I have a family and grandkids. I am retired from the Army National Guard. My word is my bond. I would never lie about anything like this, nor would my family. I have no reason to. I have told this story to numerous friends. My real friends believe me. Others scoff and roll their eyes...I saw what I saw. My family saw it...That is my story."

Zhangpo County Theater

The following account, from Chinese researcher Paul Dong, is one of very few cases in this book from outside the United States. It is also the most widely viewed UFO sighting involving an outdoor movie. Technically, it doesn't involve a drive-in theater. Instead, a crowd of 3000 people had gathered to watch an "open-air" showing of a film. By now it should come as no surprise that the theater was visited by UFOs. In this case, tragically, the consequences would be fatal.

"On the evening of 7 July 1977, at Zhangpo County in Fujian Province of East China," Dong writes, "more than 3000 people were watching an open-air showing of the Romanian film, *Along the Danube Delta*, at the commune playground. Around 8:30 p.m., a section of the audience suddenly spotted two large, oblate, orange-colored, luminous objects descending toward the crowd. The objects continued their descent and passed so low over the spectators that they almost hit the ground. They emitted a vivid glow around them and flew only a few meters apart, and so close to the people that heat could be felt and a humming sound was heard. Panic spread and people threw themselves to the ground in fright, trampling two children to death and injuring more than 300 others. After passing so low over the melee, the two UFOs ascended rapidly again and disappeared into the night sky above, streaking away in seconds."

In his article, "The China Airport Sighting -- Just One in China's Long UFO History," researcher Marcus Lowth writes about the famous Zhangpo sighting. "Despite the multiple witnesses, and the horrific response the sighting evoked, Chinese authorities initially suspected some kind of 'optical stunt' by the cinema. They would insist on studying the film and the building. They examined all aspects of the footage and failed to find any evidence to back up their claims. The sighting remains unexplained."

Later, the film was aired again "under the same atmospheric conditions." This time nothing "abnormal" occurred.

Wisconsin Drive-In Theater

Given the huge number of drive-in UFO encounters, there must be many thousands of people who have seen UFOs at drive-ins. In this next case, the witness estimates that there were at least 300 people.

It was the summer of 1977, and Anthony S. and his family were attending a drive-in theater in southeastern Wisconsin to watch a double-feature.

Says Anthony, "During the middle of the second movie, a very large disc, or flying saucer, emerged from the horizon and hovered about fifty feet above the screen for about five minutes...Everyone saw it...people were honking their horns, flashing their lights, and running to the snack center to use the phones. The next day, my mother made several calls to report the incident, but was not taken seriously by anyone. Not only that, I never heard a word about the sighting from anywhere or anyone. It was undeniable..."

Anthony still remembers the name of the theater, exactly where it occurred, and the names of both movies. He has withheld this information in the hopes of locating new witnesses who were there that night and could corroborate the events. *Anyone?*

Federal Way Drive-In Theater

While drive-in UFO encounters are fairly common, only rarely do they actually affect the movie itself. This next case is a good example, and would be classified under the Hynek system as a close encounter of the second kind.

Around 1977-1978, six-year-old "Stephan," his brother and their parents went to a drive-in theater in Federal Way, Washington. They parked their Volkswagen Beetle in front of the screen and began to watch an old black-and-white movie, which Stephan found somewhat boring. He doesn't remember the movie, but he will never forget what happened next.

"During the movie," Stephan says, "the screen went all fuzzy and everyone was honking. Then, just along the trees above the theater, a large object was hovering above us. As a child, it looked enormous and had lots of lights circling around it. There was no sound of engine or anything. It was right above us, so there was no mistaking the massive object...It hovered for about thirty seconds or so, and then it shot off instantaneously and was gone behind the row of trees. After it left, the movie came back on clear and was no longer fuzzy. It was sort of like a scene out of *The Twilight Zone*, with the effect on the movie screen and all. My mom, dad and older brother all saw the same thing, so I know it wasn't a kid's imagination. Even to this day, and despite being a young kid, the memory is ingrained in my mind."

Century 4 Drive-In Theater

By now, the pattern of drive-in theater encounters is firmly established. In case after case, the same sequence of events occurs: a UFO approaches at low level over a theater, in full view of all the movie-goers, often hovering in place, sometimes putting on a little show for the witnesses. This next case is no exception.

On May 7, 1978, a family of four went to the Century 4 Drive-in Theater in Grand Prairie, Texas to watch a documentary film called *Beyond and Back*. The film was about life after death. Little did they know, they were about to see something from beyond Earth.

There were four screens, with a total capacity of 2000 cars.

Tim (age ten) was outside of the car when the UFO arrived. "I noticed people flashing headlights and honking. I then noticed people getting out of their cars."

"Oh, my God!" his mom shouted. "Do you see that?"

"Yes," Tim's father and brother chorused. Tim quickly glanced up where they were looking. Unfortunately, the object was already gone. His family described seeing a silent triangular-shaped object about the size of three football fields. It was covered with colored lights, and was hovering in place. Just before Tim looked up, it darted off at high speed, and in less than three seconds, was so high up in the sky it looked like a star.

Although there was a military base nearby, none of the witnesses felt that the object was conventional. As Tim says, "I know this sighting was real. We still talk about it almost thirty years later."

The theater later added a screen and became the Century Five Drive-In. Unfortunately, it was right before the sudden decline in popularity. In 1987, the theater was closed down and demolished.

Chula Vista Drive-In Theater

Some drive-in encounters have levels of mystery that still remain unsolved. A few weeks after the above incident, on May 27, 1978, dozens of calls poured into the Police Department and Sheriff's Station in Chula Vista, California. The calls were in regard to a large object which was hovering next to the Chula Vista drive-in theater. The witnesses were put in touch with investigators, however, when the investigators arrived the witnesses were strangely unwilling to talk.

The main investigator was Peter Schlesinger. "They wouldn't talk to us," he says. "They just stared at us blankly, like zombies."

Schlesinger talked to several others who observed the object. Most were badly frightened by its appearance. When Schlesinger heard that four police officers also observed the craft from the station roof, he arranged an interview. However, when he went to meet them the next day, all four officers had been transferred.

Two were moved from their residences. The other two, he learned, were no longer employees of the Chula Vista Police. Three years later, Schlesinger tracked down one of the officers in Montana. The officer, however, still refused to acknowledge the incident. Schlesinger speculates that they were either threatened or paid off to keep silent about the encounter.

Blue Ridge Drive-In Theater

Another case in which a UFO actually affected the movie itself occurred around July 1978. "Caleb" and his best friend were both ten-years-old when his mother took them to the Blue Ridge Drive-In Theater in Saylorsburg, Pennsylvania. It was a double-feature, (not counting the UFO!)

During the second movie, around midnight, the small wired window-speaker suddenly became increasingly full of static, to the point that it became un-listenable. At that moment, a large, dark, oval-shaped object appeared overhead. The moon was out that night, and they could clearly see the object, which appeared to have strange spokes around it.

"It was fairly quiet," Caleb said, "but there was a low-level hum. The craft passed directly over the huge outdoor movie screen, and the movie projection became distorted. The craft continued to move slowly away, and the projection cleared up, and the speakers cleared up. At that point, I would say about a dozen cars turned on their headlights and left the drive-in, as did we."

About fifteen years later, Caleb had a chance encounter with his best friend, who was now a school principal. "Do you remember when we were in the drive-in theater?" he asked, and was about to mention the strange object they had seen. Before Caleb could finish, his friend blurted out, "UFO!"

Albion Drive-In Theater

A great case from 1978 comes from Nick Collier, who responded to my Facebook request for people to share their encounters at drive-in theaters. His experience is a wonderful example of a brazen UFO fearlessly showing itself off to a captive audience.

The Albion Drive-In Theater (now demolished) was located in a large field off Interstate 94 in Albion, Michigan, a small town of about 11,000 residents. The theater itself held up to 400 cars. It was located on a rural lot. As Nick says, "Nothing but a large corn field. In the middle of the field sat an extremely old and large oak tree." This fact would soon become important.

Nick recalls that it was a Friday night in the summertime of 1978. "The place was packed, as usual," he says. "While watching the first movie, I noticed an object sitting over that tree out in the cornfield. It had to have been big, considering the distance. It was a classic saucer-shape, lights running around the center, and one [light] on top illuminated the object."

Nick's brother was in the National Guard. He should know what the object might be. Nick alerted his brother to the object. "What's that?" he asked.

"It's a helicopter," his brother replied glancing at it. But then he took a second look.

Says Nick, "Then he froze, looked at it again. Our windows were down. You'd have heard a helicopter. We both got out of the car. The whole drive-in started getting out of their cars. The concession-stand employees and customers came out and stood there. We all watched this thing just hovering, watching us. This lasted maybe a few seconds, then, like nothing any of us had seen, it went straight up at incredible speed and turned into a white dot and vanished. Everyone stood around silent for a second, and then startled conversation broke out."

The man in the car next to them shouted out, "Damn, I guess them things are real!"

Despite the huge number of witnesses, and the excited conversation that followed, the next day it was a different story. Nick checked the local newspaper, expecting to read about the incident, but was surprised to see it wasn't mentioned. "There was nothing in the *Albion Evening Recorder* the next day," he says. "Most of the townsfolk never talked about it afterward."

Years later, he still remembers the incident vividly. "It was the first time I'd ever seen what I consider an unidentified flying object...My brother and I still talk about it."

Today the theater is gone, and the old oak tree where the object hovered has died and been removed. Whenever he can, Nick passes by the location of the sighting. As he says, "I always take that exit because of that incident, believe it or not."

Southwest Twin Drive-In Theater

Is it a coincidence that so many UFOs are hovering near drive-ins? This next case, from "Christopher" of Memphis Tennessee, shows that in some cases, UFOs are specifically attracted to the drive-in theater itself. While some cases are random fly-bys, more often it is not a coincidence. Drive-in movie theaters are definitely "UFO attractors."

"My story begins with a phone call from my best friend on Sunday morning, April 14, [1979], writes Christopher. "He was excited, and related the sighting he had witnessed the previous night while at the Southwest Twin Drive-in Theater. He said he had noticed people getting out of their cars at one point during the movie, and looking up at the sky. He did likewise and saw four red lights moving over the drive-in, in a square or diamond formation. After the UFOs hovered silently over the drive-in for a few minutes, they suddenly departed at great speed in four different directions."

Fountain Valley Drive-In Theater

It was the summer of 1980. "Tony" was seventeen years old and about to become a senior. One August evening, Tony and his girlfriend went to see a drive-in movie near their home in Fountain Valley, California. Little did they know, they were about to experience one of the most memorable evenings of their lives.

"During the movie," says Tony, "I became distracted from the screen by a cluster of disc-shaped objects that were moving in ways that we don't see aircraft move, with extreme speeds, abrupt stops, and pulsating, glowing yellow-orange lights."

The objects were in their line of sight, above and to the left of the movie screen. Tony pointed out the objects to his girlfriend, who described exactly what Tony was seeing.

"We both watched them in amazement," says Tony. "And then in an instant, they shot up and were gone. Right after this occurred, the city power went out. We sat in darkness, talking, waiting for the movie to come on and wondering if our 'neighbors' in cars near us also saw what we observed. Honestly, it was so shocking. We were only seventeen, and we thought they would think we were crazy. So, we didn't ask anyone."

But the sighting wasn't over yet. "About 10-15 minutes later, the power returned and the movie resumed," says Tony. "Shortly after the movie resumed, a larger craft appeared, with the same disc-shape and pulsating yellow orange lights. [It made] the same bizarre movements and ultimately shot up and disappeared as the previous cluster did."

At that point, the power went off again. And when it didn't come back on, the theater sent everyone home.

Tony was left rattled by the experience. He drove his girlfriend to her home, and then phoned his mom, telling her about the sightings, and that he was too frightened to drive any further that night. Instead he spent the night at his girlfriend's house.

"I did not believe in UFOs before this occurred," Tony explains. "I thought it was a ridiculous creation on the cover of *Enquirer* magazine."

Hollowbrook Drive-In Theater

The huge number of sightings over drive-ins is clearly no coincidence. One summer evening in 1981, a resident of Waterbury, Connecticut stepped out of his home and was shocked to see a huge disc hovering right over his house. "It had light around the edges and was completely silent," he said. "It hovered for a short time, and then swooped off so fast you could hardly see it go."

The witness tried to chase it in his car, but within seconds, the object was a distant star-like object high above. Later, the witness received remarkable corroboration of his sighting when the local newspaper, the *Waterbury Republican-American,* ran a column about local UFO sightings, saying that they had received about 800 calls, and that the UFO had visited the local drive-in theater.

Skeptics later said that an advertising balloon from *Bob's Surplus Store* caused the sightings, an explanation which the witness calls, "what a joke!"

This was around the beginning of a wave of local sightings which came to be known as the Hudson Valley UFO wave. It wasn't long after the above incident that another drive-in encounter occurred near the same area. In this case, the behavior of the UFO was shockingly fearless. It was around 1982-1983 and Oscar [pseudonym] was at the Hollowbrook Drive-In at Cortlandt, New York. Oscar describes what happened:

"There was a large crowd of people watching the movie. From directly behind the screen appeared a huge chevron-shaped craft with many white and orange lights along the forward edges. People instantly started yelling and screaming while pointing to it. Several cars started and drove quickly and erratically out of the drive-in lot."

Oscar heard some of the witnesses say that the objects were ultra-light planes. But having seen the ultra-lights previously, Oscar knew that this object was not a group of planes.

This object, says Oscar, was "exceedingly different" and moved steadily, and so slowly that a jogger could have practically kept up with it. It was about 200-300 feet wide. It had huge lights 20-30 feet wide and a smaller red light in the center. Oscar estimates that hundreds of people saw the object as it moved over the theater and toward the town of Peekskill. After the event, he never heard another word about it. At the time, other local sightings were beginning to grab the headlines.

Edgewood Drive-In Theater

The vast majority of drive-in UFO encounters occurred from the 1950s through the 1970s. As time marched on, drive-in theaters across the United States began to close down. This logically resulted in a significant reduction of drive-in theater UFO encounters. However, despite this, cases still continued to occur.

Around 1983, a UFO was seen hovering over the Edgewood Drive-in Theater in Baldwin Park, California. With a capacity of 2000 cars, it was one of the larger theaters around. At least two independent witnesses claim to have been there.

One of the witnesses was there with his entire family. "It's an experience the four of us will never forget," he says. "A strange bright craft hovering near the upper right corner of the projector screen for almost two full minutes before disappearing at such a rapid rate that one would miss its departure in the blink of an eye. The drive-in was almost full. I remember folks panicking and fleeing the theater."

The witness posted the case on an internet website in the hopes of locating other witnesses. It took six years, but finally another witness stepped forward.

"I was there that night with the UFO," says the new witness. "I remember it well. I remember like 70-80 percent of the cars headed like crazy out the exit...everyone [was] freaking out. At first it seemed like a helicopter, but as it got to the screen, there was no way it was a helicopter. Also, it didn't make any noise."

Spokane Drive-In Theater

It was the summer of 1993. Charles had just graduated from his junior year in high school. He decided to take his girlfriend to the local theater in Spokane, Washington to see the wildly popular movie, *Jurassic Park*. It was a clear night except for a large thunder cloud approaching from the north as Charles parked his Datsun 310 backward in his spot, opened up the hatchback and lay down to watch the movie with his girlfriend.

"The opening credits started rolling," Charles said, "and I was concerned about the storm approaching…I'm watching the storm because I didn't want it to ruin the movie. When I looked up at the clouds, an orange orb came out of the clouds, kind of at an angle. The first thing that came to my mind was, 'What the f**k is that?'"

The object glowed yellowish orange. "I think it was bigger than a car," says Charles, "probably between the size of an airplane and a car. It was hard to judge how far away it was. It was obviously between the drive-in and the mountains, but other than a rough guess of three to five miles, I can't say…it travelled at an angle with incredible, yet constant speed, and then stopped on a dime. That all happened in maybe a quarter-second -- super-fast.

"When it stopped, I squinted at it. I thought, 'What the f**k is that?' Right about that time…it shot off to the horizon toward the sunset. It literally moved so fast, I could barely trace the direction that it went. If I hadn't been facing the right direction, I might not have known which way it went. But it did go slow enough that I could trace it with my eyes. When it shot off, I sat there for two minutes dumbfounded, in shock. I couldn't believe what I saw."

Various theories bounced around in his head. It couldn't be a reflection, as both he and his girlfriend weren't looking through the windshield. There were no telephone wires, no trees. "There was nothing," said Charles, "just plain sky and the object."

Charles was convinced that they saw something unusual. Following the incident, and thinking that many other people must have seen it, he tried to find some mention of it in newspapers. He found nothing to corroborate his encounter.

"The moral of the story," says Charles, "this happened in a city with over 200,000 people and I'm the only one to see it and talk about it online. This could be happening in cities all over America and ninety-nine percent of people will not see it because they're not looking. So how can you be so sure UFOs don't exist?"

Charles was left permanently changed by the encounter. He wrote about his experience on a blog post titled, *Let Me Tell You About the Time I Saw a UFO at the Drive-In*.

"To this day," he writes, "I can't tell you if it was an alien or not, but I've never seen, heard or had anybody describe something that exists that is what I saw that evening. Period."

Wellfleet Drive-In Theater

By the 1990s, drive-in theaters had become almost extinct. Nevertheless, a few scattered encounters continued to occur.

In 1996, a couple was at the Wellfleet Drive-In Theater in Wellfleet, Massachusetts (now the last surviving drive-in on Cape Cod) when they decided to get out of their car to stretch their legs. At that moment, they saw "a dark triangular-shaped object" with green lights on the sides and front, pass silently overhead. As soon as it was gone, two more objects appeared and passed overhead.

"Since we were the only ones standing outside our car, I don't know if there were other witnesses," the wife said.

A lucky chance sighting? Perhaps. In this next case it appears that the theater was specifically targeted.

South Bay Drive-In Theater

Back in May of 1978, the police received a flood of calls reporting UFOs over the drive-in theater in Chula Vista, California. Almost thirty years later, the UFOs returned to the same city for an encore performance. As with other drive-in theater encounters, it was dramatic enough to draw the attention of the United States Air Force.

On July 27, 2007, an unmarried couple, (both employees of the Army and Navy base in San Diego,) were at the South Bay Drive-In in Chula Vista watching *The Simpsons Movie* when they saw a "bright light" appear to the east. They both grabbed each other and stared in awe.

Says the girlfriend, "I saw a round, disc-like object with blue lights around it, around 10-15 feet in diameter floating to the left of us. We saw it for approximately ten seconds, and it zipped away in the most odd, quick zigzag motion I've ever seen. And then it shot up going faster than anything I'd ever seen before, and it disappeared into the sky. Less than three minutes later, there were three army helicopters flying over us -- so loud that everyone around us could not hear the movie. I'm sure I'm not the only one who saw it. There must have been 100 people at the drive-in movie."

Clearfield Drive-In Theater

As the long list of cases begins to come to a close, it becomes impossible to deny that UFOs have an interest in drive-in movie theaters. Another compelling and recent case comes from an engaged couple in Clearfield, Pennsylvania.

On August 15, 2008, Marilyn (pseudonym) and her fiancé were watching a double feature at the Clearfield Drive-In. During the intermission they noticed a "strange strobing light" high in the sky. It looked like a star at first, but then it started to move. Marilyn told her husband to look, but he dismissed her claims until the object started to drop down from the sky and move "much closer." Suddenly it was right overhead.

"What we could now see was that it had a triangular-shape," Marilyn says, "with a light on each of its three corners and two red lights on its back."

They watched the object glide overhead and move out of view. Twenty minutes later, it returned. On both occasions, it was close enough that they could hear "a dull humming."

The object moved upward and then remained in place hovering for "a good period" of time.

Was it watching the movie? Marilyn isn't sure, but she knows the craft was unusual. "We were both genuinely stunned to witness such a thing."

Wilmington Drive-In Theater

One possible reason for drive-in theater encounters is that the UFO occupants are there to watch the movie. Whether for their own entertainment or to study us, perhaps they are simply interested in our films. Consider this next case in which the UFO stayed in view for the entire length of the movie.

In August or September of 2004, Joe Gingerich decided to go see the movie, *Maleficent*, at the Wilmington Drive-In Theater, in Wilmington, Ohio. While the theater was able to accommodate 500 cars, Joe estimates that there were somewhere between 100-200. At some point during the movie, a brilliant light appeared above the theater.

"Everyone there saw it," Joe says. "The whole drive-in saw a bright light that could've been mistaken for a plane, but then it shot way up high. Then it stayed in place, looking like a star for the rest of the night. Pretty crazy."

For those who want their own drive-in UFO encounter, the Wilmington Drive-in is still in operation.

Las Vegas Drive-In Theater

While only a few modern cases of drive-in theater encounters exist, they show the same exact patterns of earlier encounters.

On October 13, 2010, two friends were watching a movie at a drive-in theater in Las Vegas, Nevada. There were multiple screens playing different movies. Suddenly one of the friends gasped and shouted, "What is that?"

Looking where his friend was pointing, directly above the movie screen showing their movie, the witness saw "a V-shaped object with circular lights on its underside." The object was descending slowly. As it moved behind the movie screen, it appeared to transform from a "V" shape to a "W" shape. It emerged from behind the screen and was about to move behind the next screen when it suddenly faded away.

Says the witness, "It looked as if it activated some sort of cloaking mechanism that appeared otherworldly and frankly, unnerving."

Both friends were shocked. They don't know if anybody else saw it, but they felt that probably there were other witnesses as "the craft was quite noticeable..."

Autorama Drive-In Theater

A remarkably similar event to the above case occurred on May 22, 2011, at the Autorama Drive-in Theater in North Ridgeville, Ohio. One witness describes what happened: "Around the beginning of the movie, we saw about 5-6 round lights appear to the right of the movie screen...really close, not much higher up than the screen...They all seemed to float together, staying about the same distance apart and went behind the movie screen, then to the left of it...You could hear other people saying things, 'What are those strange lights?' We tried to take a picture, but it didn't come out. Other people were taking pictures."

After a few moments, the lights "faded to small lights, then nothing." Thinking that many people must have reported the sighting, the witness checked the newspapers the next day, but there was no mention of any UFOs.

The witness never forgot his encounters, and years later reported the sighting to MUFON. Writes the witness, "I am so a believer now!"

Wicksburg Drive-In Theater

Is it possible that a UFO can hover in front of a crowded drive-in and be seen by only a few people? Evidently, yes. This next case is a good example.

On March 30, 2013, two friends (both aviation enthusiasts) went to the local drive-in theater in Wicksburg, Alabama. Suddenly one of them shouted out, "What the heck is that?"

They both looked and saw a line of square windows attached to an object that was only detectable because of the windows and the fact that it was blocking out the stars behind it.

Says the witness, "It matched the dark sky perfectly with no reflection, none...when I saw this, I knew it was way different than anything I'd ever seen, so I got out of my truck as fast as I could, to watch and listen for noise. Not a sound."

The object appeared to be disc-shaped and at a very low altitude. Shortly after they saw it, it accelerated away at high speed. "Nothing moves that fast without making some noise," said the witness.

They looked around them in disbelief. There were at least 200 people watching the movie, and yet, nobody else seemed to see it. Despite this, both witnesses are convinced they saw something unexplained.

"What we saw that night was beyond anything both of us could comprehend or understand," the witness says. "The only word either one of us could come up with was 'incredible.' There is nothing man-made, that I know of, that can do what I saw done that night. We do not have that kind of technology. Incredible!"

Mansfield Drive-In Theater

As we have seen, some drive-in UFO encounters appear to be a simple matter of being in the right place at the right time. On August 10, 2014, a man and woman were watching *The Guardians of the Galaxy* at the Mansfield Drive-in Theater in Mansfield, Connecticut for the second time when they noticed a "bright, orange glowing object" move slowly across the sky.

It was too low to be a satellite, and clearly wasn't a plane or helicopter. They watched it for a few minutes as it moved slowly across the sky. Realizing that they were unable to identify it, they quickly tried to film it with their phone. At that moment, the object disappeared.

Whatever the explanation, it inspired the witnesses to purchase a "travel telescope" just in case there was a repeat appearance.

Knights Action Park

Drive-ins are clearly a great place to see UFOs. Another exciting case occurred on July 10, 2015. A married couple and their 16-year-old son were watching the latest *Terminator* movie at the Knights Action Park in Springfield, Illinois, (also known as the Route 66 Twin Drive-In Theater) when the teen-ager saw what he first thought was a shooting star darting behind the movie screen. But then the object made a swooping ninety-degree turn. It disappeared behind the screen and was gone.

Neither of his parents saw it, but the theater was crowded and he feels confident that "someone saw it too." It impressed him enough to report the sighting to NUFORC.

"I have seen shooting stars before," he said. "This was nothing like one."

Tascosa Drive-In Theater

With drive-in theaters all but extinct, the era of UFOs putting on displays over the movie screen and stealing the show seems to be largely over. This next case, from Texas, provides one of our final and most recent cases.

Angel Dee is the on-air DJ and assistant program/music director at 96.9 Kiss Radio F.M. in Amarillo, Texas. In 2015 (approx.,) Dee and her family went to the local Tascosa Drive-In theater to check out a movie. It's a large theater (still operational) with a capacity of 800 cars. It was a clear night, and Dee, always an avid sky-watcher, found herself gazing into the sky. "All of a sudden," says Dee, "a red flashing light came out of nowhere. It was super-fast! It came down and shot back up."

"Wow!" she shouted. "Did you see that?"

Although the sighting was quick, Dee's family saw the entire event.

"This thing made a ninety-degree turn and zoomed off," Dee says. "This all happened within five seconds. Yeah, it was that fast. And it was completely silent, no kind of sound at all. We were all left in awe. After that, the movie wasn't as interesting as it should have been. We all kept watching the sky."

It wasn't long before their persistence was rewarded. "The UFO soon returned," Dee says. "Now, not only was this thing extremely fast, but it was moving in angles that no aircraft could. These were sharp fast movements. I don't know what I really saw, but I am convinced it was a UFO from outer space. I was left baffled. I kept trying to come up with realistic possibilities, but the truth is, there isn't one. It was a UFO."

Dee later went public with her sighting on the radio. So far, no further witnesses have come forth.

The Tascosa drive-in was first opened in 1952. Then in 1978, a fire destroyed the north screen. It remained opened until 1994.

Then, in 1999 it was restored and re-opened. Today it is one of Texas's last remaining drive-in theaters.

Conclusions

So many drive-in UFO encounters! With more than 100 cases, it's undeniable that drive-in theaters do attract UFOs. In case after case we see objects that pose directly above or next to the drive-in screen. In most cases, the objects are extremely brazen, approaching closely and performing all kinds of extreme maneuvers above the astonished witnesses.

There are two main categories. One involves random fly-bys, and the other involves theaters that are being actively targeted by UFOs. It is this second category, of course, that we are concerned with here.

Consider this undated case from respected researcher, John P. Timmerman. In an interview in 1999, Timmerman revealed a conversation he had with a doctor, who told Timmerman about his drive-in theater encounter. Says Timmerman, "[He] told me he had had a sighting of his own...He was in one of these drive-in movies in Lima, Ohio, which was where I lived. And he said they were parked there watching the screen when a discoid object moved slowly behind and beyond -- not far away in the sky, not very high. It went behind the screen, came out the other side, and stopped, and suddenly disappeared...he said it just wasn't visible. I said, 'You mean it moved away?' He said, 'No, it just, *snap*, it wasn't there.'"

Timmerman was amazed because as the doctor described the incident, Timmerman recognized the case. As he says, "I took a report from someone else in our community who had given me, previously years ago, that same story. I'll bet they were in the same audience the same night he was."

This case has all the earmarks of other encounters, and is clearly another example of a UFO intentionally putting on a show for the witnesses. And there are still more cases. Another is contributed by "Allie", who (sometime in the 1990s) saw a UFO hover over the Sunset Drive-In in Colchester, Vermont. She doesn't remember much about the UFO itself, but she remembers that all the people at the theater saw it. "Everyone was gazing up at the sky instead of the movie," she says. "I remember people getting out of their car in an attempt to see it more clearly."

And for those who think that these types of encounters are over, here's a recent case from the Fish Creek Drive-In Theater in Fish Creek, Wisconsin. It occurred on July 4, 2017. Says the witness: "Four of us were at the drive-in at Fish Creek, in Door County. My oldest son saw the object in the sky moving very fast, and pointed the object out to the rest of us. We all saw it turn wildly in the sky and shoot off in a northerly direction for a few minutes. Suddenly it stopped and didn't move for a few seconds, and then ascended into space until it was gone."

And a final even more recent case: In the summer of 2018, a mother and her son went to the Coburg Drive-In theater in Melbourne, Australia when a bright orb the size of a basketball dropped out of the sky and hovered directly in front of the screen itself. Following the event, after the movie was over, five cars at the theater had mysteriously lost their battery power and had to be jump-started. Other people said that as they left the theater and headed home, the UFO briefly followed them along the highway.

As we have seen, not all cases show brazen UFO behavior. People who go to drive-ins put themselves in a position where they can view the night sky for hours at a time. Obviously, this increases the chances of seeing a UFO, and some cases do seem to reflect this. Most of the drive-in UFO encounters, however, involve UFOs that clearly know they are being seen, want to be seen and are putting on a show.

The targeted cases are usually very low level, long-lasting sightings. Sometimes the audience reacts by honking horns, flashing lights or sometimes panicking and fleeing the theater. In a few cases, the UFOs physically affect the movie itself. One thing the witnesses agree upon: these are very dramatic sightings, something they will remember for the rest of their lives. It gives a whole new meaning to the term "UFO screen memories."

Discarding the cases of random fly-bys, still, the question is *why*? Why are ETs targeting theaters? With their enormous screens, drive-ins do make a highly visible target, especially from above. But are the ETs there to watch the movie? Are they attracted to an audience that is in a susceptible, focused, trance-like state? Are they there to reveal themselves and their presence on Earth?

Let's take a closer look at a few of these theories.

Are they there for the movie? Several firsthand witnesses have raised this possibility, and a few cases support this theory in that the UFOs remained visible for the duration of the film, or most of it. However, in most cases, the UFOs do not remain that long, Furthermore, they often dart around, sometimes moving behind the movie screen. It's a nice theory, but I don't think it accounts for most of the cases. This would also negate the theory that UFOs are there to study the movies to learn about humans. Considering the overt violence of many movies, I certainly hope they aren't studying movies to learn about human society!

Viewed from above, drive-in theaters have a highly visible and very striking appearance. They are easily spotted and very recognizable in aerial photos. The huge triangular footprints with rows of cars and gigantic glowing screens are impossible to miss.

Perhaps then, the ETs are simply curious. UFOs do seem to be very interested in all things human. Perhaps they are simply curious about why humans are congregating in large numbers in parking lots and watching the brightly lit screens at night. From an outside perspective, this type of human behavior might seem strange.

But if this is true, couldn't ETs simply study from a distance without revealing their presence? Why would they play peek-a-boo around the movie screen? Why would they put on displays for a stunned audience? The ETs may be curious about us, but this does not explain all the elements of these types of encounters.

Are they there to abduct the audience? Do they see the audience as "easy pickings?" Perhaps, but there are only a few cases that seem to fit this scenario. The vast majority are simple sightings. Dramatic, yes, but most cases would be classified as close encounters of the first kind. I was able to locate a few cases of people who had very dramatic encounters (including a few abduction accounts) while driving home *after* having seen a drive-in movie. However, the UFO did not appear at the theater. Again, this theory doesn't really account for the evidence.

This brings us to the main theory. Are drive-in theaters being targeted by the UFOs as part of an agenda to announce their presence?

What makes drive-in movie encounters so interesting is how different they are from normal encounters. Generally speaking, UFOs are evasive and sightings are brief. UFOs that remain in full view of witnesses for a long time are relatively rare, and yet, many of the drive-in encounters last for several minutes or longer. It's almost as if the ETs are taking advantage of the fact that they have a large captive audience, but not so large that it would cause a panic. At least not in most cases! As we have seen, several of these cases have caused near riots.

Important here is, UFO drive-in encounters are not only of long duration, they are usually extremely low-level sightings. Another perhaps significant feature is that they often appear right next to the movie screen itself. They typically approach the theater and either hover in place, or put on a highly dramatic display.

Also important are the many cases involving electromagnetic effects, even to the point of shutting down the entire movie. These cases show once again that UFOs have no fear of being seen, and apparently want to be observed.

Given the unusually low level of the sightings, the fact that they appear right next to the screen, that they put on a little show, that they remain for a long duration, and the overt "look at me!" behavior of the UFOs, it seems safe to conclude that the UFOs are showing themselves intentionally and are, in effect, announcing their presence.

They are simply showing themselves in such a way that it becomes impossible for witnesses to deny that they are looking at something un-Earthly. While this is speculation, the brazen nature of these types of encounters strongly indicates that the purpose behind the agenda is to convince witnesses that UFOs are real.

If so, their agenda has been a huge success. The witnesses to these encounters now believe UFOs are real. And when it comes to influencing society, just look at the case of Peter Davenport. If he hadn't seen that UFO at that drive-in theater in St. Louis Missouri in 1953, when he was only six years old, he wouldn't be the director of NUFORC, and the entire organization may have been shut down.

Whatever the motive behind the UFOs' strong attraction to drive-in theaters, the end result is that many thousands of people have seen UFOs firsthand. And given that most people don't report their sightings, the 100 cases documented here are probably only the tip of the iceberg. Likely there are hundreds or even thousands more.

One very important factor is that none of these people are alone during their encounter. Having another witness with you who is seeing the same thing definitely helps corroborate your account. In the huge database of UFO sightings, a singular sighting being witnessed by more than a hundred people is proportionally rare. With drive-in encounters, however, this is the rule. That fact alone makes drive-in UFO encounters unique. In these cases, there are usually anywhere from 50 to 300 witnesses per event, or more. The Zhangpo encounter had a record-making 3000 witnesses. The cases in this book alone include a conservative estimate of about 20,000 witnesses.

Ultimately, drive-in theaters have apparently become an extremely efficient method for UFOs to introduce themselves and convince lots of people of their presence.

Another important fact about drive-in UFO encounters is their credibility. A long-lasting, low-level, multi-witness encounter is very difficult to debunk or deny, and makes any arguments of hoaxes, hallucinations or misperceptions completely untenable.

It's also interesting to note the regular frequency of cases. The fifties, sixties and seventies were the heyday of UFO drive-in cases, with cases occurring nearly every year. Following the 1970s, the number of drive-ins dropped dramatically, leading to a corresponding drop of related encounters.

Today, drive-in theaters are a dying breed. For that reason alone, most people today have missed that unique period in history, lasting only about three decades, in which people were treated to UFO displays put on by the ETs just for them.

Thankfully, drive-ins aren't quite dead yet. They still have a small but faithful group of fans. Also, the worldwide flu pandemic of 2020 has caused a resurgence of attendance and an increase in popularity. So, there's still a chance that more encounters will be reported. And as we have seen, with so many cases and so many witnesses, we can safely conclude that drive-ins do attract UFOs.

While these encounters are generally categorized as close encounters of the first kind, one could easily argue that they are *all* actually CE-5's. It may be accidental, but the fact is that drive-ins could be considered an effective method for initiating a UFO encounter. If you want to see a UFO, drive-ins are a good place to start. And if you're lucky, you might get to see a show that's better than the movie itself.

As we have seen, stranger things have happened.

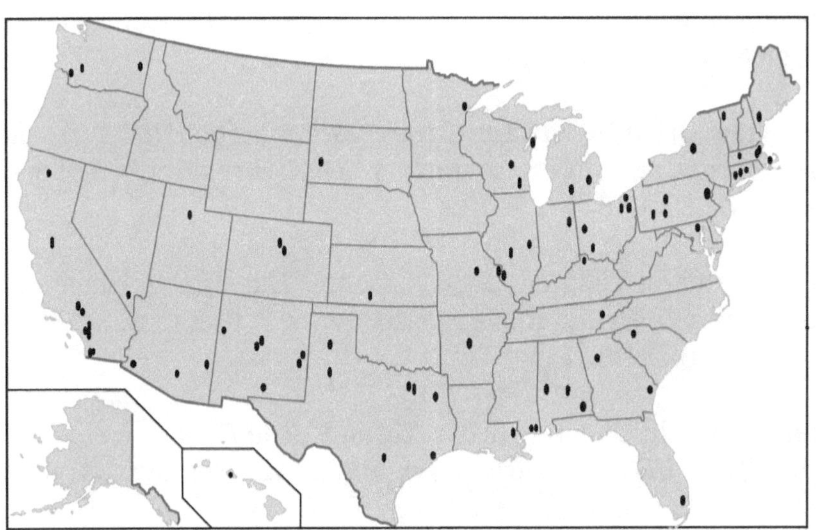

Sources

Introduction: Roybal, David. "Dead Cows Are Fair Game for News Media." *New Mexican.* Santa Fe, NM – Sep 20, 1994. (see UFONS, Mar 1995, #308, p20) https://driveintheater.com/

Starlite Drive-In Theater: Editors. "Reporter Sees Flying Thing." *The Spartanburg Journal.* Spartanburg, SC, July 24, 1950; McCullough, Alex. "Flying Something Seen Saturday." *The Spartanburg Herald.* Spartanburg, South Carolina, July 4, 1950.

Fair Park Drive-In Theater: Gross, Loren E. *The Fifth Horseman of the Apocalypse: UFOs -- A History, Aug-Dec 1950.* Fremont, CA: Loren E. Gross. C1950, p24.

Oak Ridge Drive-In Theater: Gross, Loren E. *The Fifth Horseman of the Apocalypse: UFOs -- A History, Aug-Dec 1950.* Fremont, CA: Loren E. Gross. C1950, p46.

Fair View Drive-In Theater: Gross, Loren E. *The Fifth Horseman of the Apocalypse: UFOs -- A History, 1951.* Fremont, CA: Loren E. Gross. C1983, p46.

Beach Drive-In Theater: Gross, Loren E. *The Fifth Horseman of the Apocalypse: UFOs -- A History, Jan-May 1952.* Fremont, CA: Loren E. Gross. C1982, p40.

Yuma Drive-In Theater: Gross, Loren E. *The Fifth Horseman of the Apocalypse: UFOs -- A History, Jan-May 1952.* Fremont, CA: Loren E. Gross. C1982, p40; Gross, Loren E. *The Fifth Horseman of the Apocalypse: UFOs -- A History, Aug 1952. Supplemental Notes.* Fremont, CA: Loren E. Gross. C2002, p97-98;

https://www.fold3.com/image/6313889?terms=yuma%20arizona

Universal City Drive-In Theater: Gross, Loren E. *The Fifth Horseman of the Apocalypse: UFOs -- A History, Jan-May 1952, Supplemental Notes*. Fremont, CA: Loren E. Gross. C2001, p40.

Starlight Outdoor Theater: Gross, Loren. *The Fifth Horseman of the Apocalypse -- UFOs a History, Jun-Jul 20, 1952*. Fremont, CA: Loren E. Gross, c1986. Pp11, 61; Gross, Loren. *The Fifth Horseman of the Apocalypse -- UFOs a History, Jun-Jul 20, 1952, Supplemental Notes*. Fremont, CA: Loren E. Gross, c1986. Pp11, 61; *Journal*. Rapid City, South Dakota, July 18, 1952.

Six Drive-In Theater Encounters: Gross, Loren E. *The Fifth Horseman of the Apocalypse -- UFOs: A History, Jul 21-31, 1952*, c1986, pp7, 16, 34; Gross, Loren E. *The Fifth Horseman of the Apocalypse -- UFOs: A History, Jul 21-31, 1952: Supplemental Notes*, c2001, pp15, 109; *Evening Globe*. Boston, Massachusetts, July 23, 1952; "Feature Attraction at the Drive-In Is Not a Movie." *Capital*. Sedalia, Missouri, July 30, 1952.

Terrace Drive-In Theater: Gross, Loren E. *The Fifth Horseman of the Apocalypse. UFOs: A History, Aug 1952*. Fremont, CA: Loren E. Gross, c1986, pp37-39.

Rodeo Drive-In Theater: Olson, Richard. "Pilot Reports 'Saucers' Over Tucson." *Citizen*. Tucson, AZ: Aug 14, 1952.

Family Drive-In Theater: Gross, Loren E. *The Fifth Horseman of the Apocalypse. UFOs: A History, Aug 1952*. Fremont, CA: Loren E. Gross, c1986, p45, 99; *Palm Beach Post*. West Palm Beach, FL., Aug 29, 1952.

Corral & Western Drive-In Theaters: Gross, Loren E. *The Fifth Horseman of the Apocalypse -- UFOs: A History, 1951*, c1983, pp31-32.

El Cajon Drive-In Theater: Gross, Loren E. *The Fifth Horseman of the Apocalypse. UFOs: A History, Aug 1952. Supplemental.* Fremont, CA: Loren E. Gross, c2002, pp107-108; *Tribune.* San Diego, California. Aug 18, 1952.

Yucca Drive-In Theater: Gross, Loren E. *The Fifth Horseman of the Apocalypse – UFOs: A History, Sep-Oct 1952, Supplemental Notes.* Fremont, CA: Loren E Gross, c2002. p24; *Independent.* Gallup, NM. Sep 10, 1952; Sedalia, Sep 13, 1952.

Albuquerque & Biloxi Drive-In Theaters: Gross, Loren E. *The Fifth Horseman of the Apocalypse – UFOs: A History, Sep-Oct 1952.* Fremont, CA: Loren E. Gross. C1986. P30; Gross, Loren E. *The Fifth Horseman of the Apocalypse – UFOs: A History, Sep-Oct 1952, Supplemental Notes.* Fremont, CA: Loren E Gross, c2002. P32; *Journal.* Albuquerque, New Mexico. Sep 16, 1952; National Archives of Australia, File D174, SA 5281, Adelaide Office.

Star-Lite Drive-In Theater: Gross, Loren E. *The Fifth Horseman of the Apocalypse – UFOs: A History, Sep-Oct 1952.* Fremont, CA: Loren E. Gross. C1986. P63.

Greenfield Drive-In Theater: *The APRO Bulletin.* Tucson, AZ, Vol 2, #3, Nov 15, 1953, p10.

Skyline Drive-In Theater: Davenport, Peter. https://www.spokesman.com/stories/2019/aug/10/if-you-see-a-ufo-dont-think-youre-alone-national-u/ https://www.clarionledger.com/story/magnolia/2018/08/16/look-back-charles-hickson-tells-his-abduction-ufo-miss/1006116002/ http://ufoevidence.org/news/article259.htm https://www.youtube.com/watch?time_continue=30&v=AKMF1hMYeUA&feature=emb_logo https://www.youtube.com/watch?time_continue=48&v=Qd93a3Ge_1o&feature=emb_logo

Lakeshore Drive-In Theater: Gross, Loren E. *The Fifth Horseman of the Apocalypse – UFOs: A History, Jun-Aug, 1954.* Fremont, CA: Loren E. Gross, c1990. P82.

Fort Wayne Drive-In Theater: Mutual UFO Network. MUFON CMS. https://mufoncms.com/cgi-bin/report_handler.pl?req=view_long_desc&id=17304&rnd=

Pratt Drive-In Theater: Gross, Loren E. *The Fifth Horseman of the Apocalypse. UFOs – A History, May-Jul 1956, Supplemental Notes.* Fremont, CA: Loren E. Gross, c2003. pp6, 10.

Florence Drive-In Theater: Gross, Loren E. *The Fifth Horseman of the Apocalypse – UFOs: A History, Sep-Oct, 1956.* Fremont, CA: Loren E. Gross, c1994. P14.

Oakville Drive-In Theater: Gross, Loren. E. *The Fifth Horseman of the Apocalypse – UFOs: A History, May 24 – Jul 31, 1957.* Fremont, CA: Loren E. Gross, c1996, p77.

Piedmont Drive-In Theater: "A Thing Flies over Atlanta, But What?" *Constitution.* Atlanta, Georgia. Sep 27, 1957; Gross, Loren. E. *The Fifth Horseman of the Apocalypse – UFOs: A History, Aug-Sep 1957.* Fremont, CA: Loren E. Gross, c1996, p85.

Three Way Drive-In Theater: Gross, Loren E. *The Fifth Horseman of the Apocalypse – UFOs: A History, Nov 3-5, 1957.* Fremont, CA: Loren E. Gross, c1997, p19.

King Center Drive-In Theater: Gross, Loren. E. *The Fifth Horseman of the Apocalypse – UFOs: A History, Nov 6, 1957.* Fremont, CA: Loren E Gross, c1997, pp54; *Post.* Houston, TX, Nov 6, 1957.

Waterford Drive-In Movie Theater: Gross, Loren E. *The Fifth Horseman of the Apocalypse – UFOs: A History, Jul-Sep 1959.* Fremont, CA: Loren E. Gross, c2000. P68; "Flying Discs Seen in Area: Give Bonus Show at Drive-In." *Press.* Pontiac, Michigan. August 19, 1959.

Your Drive-In Theater: Gross, Loren E. *The Fifth Horseman of the Apocalypse – UFOs: A History, Jul-Dec, 1960.* Fremont, CA: Loren E. Gross. C2003., p118; "Balls of Fire! In Sky That is!" *Longview Washington News.* Jan-Jun 1960.

Newington Drive-In Theater: Gross, Loren E. *The Fifth Horseman of the Apocalypse – UFOs: A History, Jul-Dec, 1960.* Fremont, CA: Loren E. Gross. c2003., p120; "Drive-In Has Visit from V-Shaped Spector." *Hartford Times*, Hartford, CT, Nov 12, 1960.

Tillicum Drive-In Theater: http://britishcolumbiaufos.blogspot.com/2015/03/silver-disc-shaped-ufo-at-vanderhoof.html

Charlottetown Drive-In Theater: https://rense.com//general68/hdchb.htm

Ripon Drive-In Theater: *Saucer News.* Sept 1963, Vol 19, #3.

Wellington Circle Twin Drive-In Theater: Gross, Loren E. *The Fifth Horseman of the Apocalypse: UFOs -- A History, Jan-Jun 1963.* Fremont, CA: Loren E Gross. c2005, pp66-67.

Southside Drive-In Theater: Mutual UFO Network. MUFON CMS. https://mufoncms.com/cgi-bin/report_handler.pl?req=view_long_desc&id=9129&rnd=

Richland Drive-In Theater: National UFO Reporting Center. NUFORC. http://www.nuforc.org/webreports/068/S68997.html

Atlanta Drive-In Theater: National UFO Reporting Center. NUFORC. http://www.nuforc.org/webreports/069/S69893.html

Mount Shasta Drive-In Theater: National UFO Reporting Center. NUFORC. http://www.nuforc.org/webreports/004/S04274.html

Studio Drive-In Theater:

http://the-v-factor-paranormal.blogspot.com/2013/10/large-disc-ufo-with-lights-around-edge.html

Conway Drive-In Theater: National UFO Reporting Center. NUFORC.

Mentor Drive-In Theater: National UFO Reporting Center. NUFORC. http://www.nuforc.org/webreports/083/S83640.html

Dallas Drive-In Theater: "Case #224" *CRIFO Orbit*. Cincinnati, OH, CRIFO. Vol 111, #1, April 6 1956.

Southutch Drive-In Theater: Interview with author, 2020.

Bogalusa Drive-In Theater: Mutual UFO Network. MUFON CMS. https://mufoncms.com/cgi-bin/report_handler.pl?req=view_long_desc&id=98651&rnd=

Highland Drive-In Theater: Mutual UFO Network. MUFON CMS. https://mufoncms.com/cgi-bin/report_handler.pl?req=view_long_desc&id=76482&rnd= https://verytopsecret.info/2016/05/20/ufo-sighting-in-salt-lake-city-utah-on-july-21st-1967-my-family-and-i-saw-a-flying-saucer-hover-and-then-move-at-incredible-speed-while-waiting-in-car-to-enter-a-drive-in-theater/

Duluth Drive-In Theater: https://www.fold3.com/image/6887539

Longview Drive-In Theater: Mutual UFO Network. MUFON CMS. https://mufoncms.com/cgi-bin/report_handler.pl?req=view_long_desc&id=13480&rnd=

Foothill Drive-In Theater: Mutual UFO Network. MUFON CMS. https://mufoncms.com/cgi-bin/report_handler.pl?req=view_long_desc&id=30741&rnd=

Kings Drive-In Theater: http://www.cufos.org/Data-Net/Data_Net_41_1970.pdf

Southside Drive-In Theater: https://ufomg.com/2019/01/06/ufo-sighting-in-youngstown-ohio-on-1970-06-30-000000-at-drive-in-threater-as-young-teen-with-family-everybody-at-the-drive-in-was-out-of-there-cars-pointing-and-watching-this-light-in-the-sky/

Paramount Drive-In Theater: Dennett, Preston. *Extraterrestrial Visitations: True Accounts: True Accounts of Contact.* St. Paul, MN: Llewellyn Publications, 2001, pp8-10.

Kam Drive-In Theater: National UFO Reporting Center. NUFORC. http://www.nuforc.org/webreports/060/S60951.html

Winnipeg Drive-In Theater: https://www.ufosnw.com/newsite/brass-colored-object-hovers-above-drive-inn-screen/

Fort Lauderdale Drive-In Theater: https://verytopsecret.info/2014/07/24/ufo-sighting-in-fort-lauderdale-florida-on-february-10th-1974-large-disk-shape-came-over-the-drive-in-movies/

Baltimore Drive-In Theater: Mutual UFO Network. MUFON CMS. https://mufoncms.com/cgi-bin/report_handler.pl?req=view_long_desc&id=76607&rnd=

Hinesville Drive-In Theater: http://www.abovetopsecret.com/forum/thread525580/pg19

East Park Drive-In Theater: https://www.syracusenewtimes.com/exorcist-ufo/

Ascot Park Drive-In Theater: Santa, Scott J. Interview with author. (see also: Sprague, Ryan and Micah Hanks. *Somewhere in the Skies: A Human Approach to an Alien Phenomenon.* Richard Dolan Press, 2016, pp46-41.)

Portland Twin Drive-In Theater: National UFO Reporting Center. NUFORC. http://www.nuforc.org/webreports/117/S117572.html

Belleville Drive-In Theater: Mutual UFO Network. MUFON CMS. https://mufoncms.com/cgi-bin/report_handler.pl?req=view_long_desc&id=30305&rnd=

Mile High Drive-In Theater: National UFO Reporting Center. NUFORC.

Riverside Drive-In Theater: Interview with author.

Boulder Drive-In Theater: National UFO Reporting Center. NUFORC.

Yuma Drive-In Theater: http://www.openminds.tv/arizona-witness-recalls-saucer-ufo-low-drive-movie/30179

Twin Drive-In Theater: National UFO Reporting Center. NUFORC.

Zhangpo County Theater: Dong, Paul. *UFOs over Modern China.* Tucson, AZ: UFO Photo Archives, 1983, pp11, 93.

Wisconsin Drive-In Theater: http://www.ufowisconsin.com/county/reports/r1977_xxxx_unknown.html

Federal Way Drive-In Theater: National UFO Reporting Center. NUFORC. http://www.nuforc.org/webreports/133/S133796.html

Century 4 Drive-In Theater: National UFO Reporting Center. NUFORC. http://www.nuforc.org/webreports/055/S55578.html

Chula Vista Drive-In Theater: Canlen, Brae, "Maybe What You Saw Was A UFO." *Reader.* San Diego, CA – Feb 8, 1990. (See UFONS, April 1990, No #249.)

Blue Ridge Drive-In Theater:
http://ufonewshub.com/ufo-sighting-in-easton-pennsylvania-on-1978-06-30-000000-spoked-craft-slowly-passed-over-the-blue-ridge-drive-in-theatre-around-midnight-july-of-1978/
https://verytopsecret.info/2017/10/02/ufo-sighting-in-easton-pennsylvania-on-1978-06-30-000000-spoked-craft-slowly-passed-over-the-blue-ridge-drive-in-theatre-around-midnight-july-of-1978/

Albion Drive-In Theater: Interview with author.

Southwest Twin Drive-In Theater:
https://mufoncms.com/cgi-bin/report_handler.pl?req=view_long_desc&id=59427&rnd=

Fountain Valley Drive-In Theater: Mutual UFO Network. MUFON CMS.
https://mufoncms.com/cgi-bin/report_handler.pl?req=view_long_desc&id=83556&rnd=

Hollowbrook Drive-In Theater: Mutual UFO Network. MUFON CMS.
https://mufoncms.com/cgi-bin/report_handler.pl?req=view_long_desc&id=7348&rnd=

Edgewood Drive-In Theater: National UFO Reporting Center. NUFORC.

Spokane Drive-In Theater: https://97rockonline.com/let-me-tell-you-about-the-time-i-saw-a-ufo-at-the-drive-in/

Wellfleet Drive-In Theater: National UFO Reporting Center. NUFORC.

South Bay Drive-In Theater: National UFO Reporting Center. NUFORC. http://www.nuforc.org/webreports/065/S65711.html

Clearfield Drive-In Theater: National UFO Reporting Center. NUFORC. http://www.nuforc.org/webreports/065/S65249.html

Wilmington Drive-In Theater. Interview with author.

Las Vegas Drive-In Theater: National UFO Reporting Center. NUFORC. http://www.nuforc.org/webreports/078/S78360.html

Autorama Drive-In Theater: Mutual UFO Network. MUFON CMS. https://mufoncms.com/cgi-bin/report_handler.pl?req=view_long_desc&id=29394&rnd=

Wicksburg Drive-In Theater: Mutual UFO Network. MUFON CMS. https://mufoncms.com/cgi-bin/report_handler.pl?req=view_long_desc&id=46592&rnd=

Mansfield Drive-In Theater: Mutual UFO Network. MUFON CMS. https://mufoncms.com/cgi-bin/report_handler.pl?req=view_long_desc&id=60232&rnd=

Knight Actions Park: National UFO Reporting Center. NUFORC. http://www.nuforc.org/webreports/120/S120290.html

Tascosa Drive-In Theater: https://kissfm969.com/angel-dee-sees-ufo-in-amarillo-video/

Conclusions: https://www.youtube.com/watch?v=IKIjoMJXgdc&feature=youtu.be&fbclid=IwAR1TOW5pvW8hBe1iyh0FYf43q9DT0tiQO_cNfS7Ms_mbeYeQcX2pJFXRLTY
https://verytopsecret.info/2017/07/09/ufo-sighting-in-fish-creek-wisconsin-on-2017-07-04-000000-moved-very-fast-turned-very-sharp-without-changing-speed-ascended-to-space/

About the Author

Preston Dennett began investigating UFOs and the paranormal in 1986 when he discovered that his family, friends and co-workers were having dramatic unexplained encounters. Since then, he has interviewed hundreds of witnesses and investigated a wide variety of paranormal phenomena. He is a field investigator for the Mutual UFO Network (MUFON,) a ghost hunter, a paranormal researcher, and the author of dozens of books and more than 100 articles on UFOs and the paranormal. His articles have appeared in numerous magazines including *Fate, Atlantis Rising, MUFON UFO Journal, Nexus, Paranormal Magazine, UFO Magazine, Mysteries Magazine, Ufologist* and others. His writing has been translated into several different languages including German, French, Italian, Portuguese, Russian, and Icelandic. Several of his books have been Amazon UFO bestsellers. He has appeared on numerous radio and television programs, including *Coast-to-Coast* and the History Channel's *Deep Sea UFOs* and *UFO Hunters*. His research has been presented in the *LA Times,* the *LA Daily News*, the *Dallas Morning News* and other newspapers. He has taught classes on various paranormal subjects and lectures across the United States. He currently resides in southern California.

www.prestondennett.weebly.com

prestonufo@gmail.com

Books by Preston Dennett

Aliens and UFOs	Chelsea House, 2008
Bigfoot, Yeti and other Apemen	Chelsea House, 2009
California Ghosts	Schiffer Publishing, 2004
The Coronado Island UFO Incident	Galde Press, 2007
Extraterrestrial Visitations	Llewellyn Publications, 2001
Ghosts of Greater Los Angeles	Schiffer Publishing, 2010
The Healing Power of UFOs	Blue Giant Books, 2019
Human Levitation	Schiffer Publishing, 2007
Inside UFOs	Blue Giant Books, 2017
Not from Here: Volume One	Blue Giant Books, 2016
Not from Here: Volume Two	Blue Giant Books, 2017
Not from Here: Volume Three	Blue Giant Books, 2018
Onboard UFO Encounters	Blue Giant Books, 2020
One in Forty: the UFO Epidemic	Kroshka Books, 1997
Out-of-Body Exploring	Hampton Roads, 2004
Schoolyard UFO Encounters	Blue Giant Books, 2019
Supernatural California	Schiffer Publishing, 2007
UFO Healings	Wild Flower Press, 1996
UFOs at the Drive-In	Blue Giant Books, 2020
UFOs over Arizona	Schiffer Publishing, 2016
UFOs over California	Schiffer Publishing, 2005
UFOs over Colorado	Schiffer Publishing, 2017
UFOs over Nevada	Schiffer Publishing, 2014
UFOs over New Mexico	Schiffer Publishing, 2012
UFOs over New York	Schiffer Publishing, 2008
UFOs over Topanga Canyon	Llewellyn Publications, 1999
Undersea UFO Base	Blue Giant Books, 2018

Blue Giant Books
ISBN:9781653842186
226 pages

Onboard UFO Encounters

Onboard UFO Encounters contains fifteen all new original cases of people who have been taken onboard a UFO. None have been published before. What really happens when someone is taken onboard an alien craft? The answer may surprise you. These true firsthand accounts provide an extensive exploration deep into the heart of the UFO phenomenon, and show just how fascinating and strange UFO contact can be. Fifteen true accounts, told in the witnesses' own words. An onboard UFO encounter is the ultimate UFO experience.

- After being abducted by aliens, a young man continues to see grays, and later learns he has a daughter who lives among the stars.
- A woman wakes up to find herself onboard a UFO where she helps to rescue people from a horrific disaster.
- Taken onboard a UFO as a child, a marine officer stationed at Camp Pendleton encounters reptilian humanoids working with the military.
- An Air Force Officer who works for Special Forces is taken by the grays.
- A little girl realizes that the monsters in her closet are real. They are grays, who heal her and issue dire warnings for all humankind.
- A California man is invited to leave Earth and live with the ETs. Will he accept the invitation?
- An entertainer takes a road-trip across the Canadian Rockies, resulting in a shocking UFO encounter, and the realization that he is a contactee.
- After several fully conscious abductions by grays, a woman learns how to resist being taken.
- A family drives by a strange-looking "spaceship house" and decide to stop and investigate. To their amazement, they are taken inside.
- A young boy is taken for a three-hour ride onboard a UFO by friendly human-looking ETs.
- Two brothers are taken onboard a UFO, causing unforeseen consequences that will affect them both for the rest of their lives.
- A woman who works for the Army Department of Defense is approached by a UFO with a message that will save her life.
- After several missing time incidents, a young man from Louisiana remembers what happened to him when he was taken onboard a UFO.
- Seeing the cover of *Communion*, a nurse can no longer deny that she's an abductee. And one of the grays wants to talk to her about it.
- A man from England is repeatedly taken onboard a UFO. The problem is, the grays can no longer control him. Now he's ready to fight.

Why are the ETs visiting our planet? What is their agenda? Are they friendly or hostile? The answers are here.

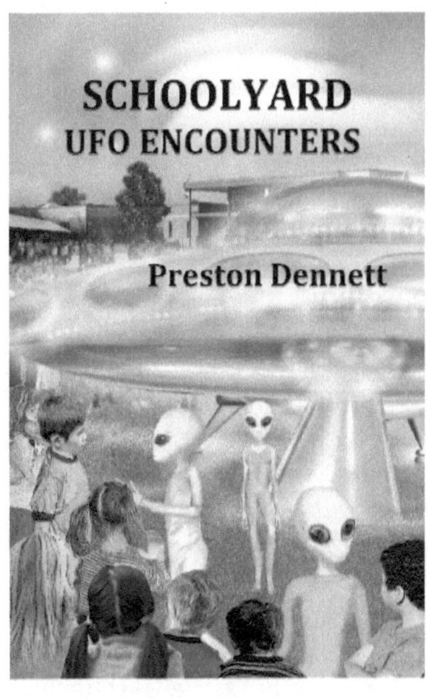

Blue Giant Books
ISBN: 9781075776984
238 pages

Schoolyard UFO Encounters

Aliens at school! Extraterrestrials on the playground!

For the past 170 years, schools across the United States and the world have been targeted and visited by UFOs. These are not simple fly-overs. In these cases, the objects hover for long periods at extremely low elevation, often landing next to the school. In many cases, humanoids are seen. Elementary schools, junior high and high schools, colleges and universities -- all have been targeted. The ETs are here, and they are coming for our children.

- March 15, 1950, thirty-one students at Prestonburg Elementary School, in Prestonburg, Kentucky observe a fleet of UFOs.
- Summer, 1952, dozens of students at Elder Park Elementary School in Glasgow, Scotland see a metallic saucer hover 30 feet above the school.
- October 22, 1955, sixty students at Jerome Elementary School in Marysville, Ohio observe a dramatic UFO display, including physical evidence in the form of angel hair.
- March 21, 1966, eighty-seven students at Hillsdale College, in Hillsdale, Michigan observe a UFO land in front of the school.
- April 6, 1966, more than 200 students at Westall High School, in Melbourne, Australia, observe three or four UFOs, one of which lands next to the school.
- April 7, 1967, more than 200 students at Crestview Elementary School in Opa-locka, Florida, observe a UFO land next to the school.
- March 17, 1970, more than 400 students at Richmond School in Maraenui, New Zealand observe a UFO hover overhead.
- February 4, 1977, fourteen students at Broad Haven Elementary School in Haverfordwest, South Wales encounter a landed UFO with occupants.
- September 16, 1994, more than 62 students at Ariel Elementary School in Ruwa, Zimbabwe observe a landed UFO with occupants.

And this is just the beginning. This unique and groundbreaking book documents more than 100 cases of schoolyard UFO encounters. Why are extraterrestrials hovering over and landing next to schools? Why are the ETs so interested in our children? Schoolyard UFO Encounters answers all these questions and more. Something very profound is happening here.

Blue Giant Books
ISBN #97817929866208
541 Pages

THE HEALING POWER OF UFOS

300 True Accounts of People Healed by Extraterrestrials

Are ETs healing humans? The answer, of course, is yes! In this landmark book, The Healing Power of UFOs, leading UFO researcher, Preston Dennett, presents a fascinating compilation of more than 300 cases of people who have been healed by extraterrestrials. Supported by firsthand eye-witness testimonies, stretching back more than 100 years to the present day, coming from across the United States and the world, this book proves that healing humans is one of the primary alien agendas on our planet. Verified by doctors and leading UFO researchers, the UFO healing cases represent incontrovertible evidence of UFO reality. Preston Dennett has been documenting and researching healing cases for more than 25 years and is the world's leading expert on UFO healing accounts. This landmark book is the culmination of his research and settles the question once and for all that medical healings as the result of a UFO encounter do actually happen. The healings include a wide variety of conditions. Injuries and flesh wounds, colds, flues and infections, serious diseases--all have been cured by ETs. Inside you will find:
• More than 70 healings of injuries.
• More than 50 healings of colds, minor illnesses and ailments.
• More than 120 healings of serious illnesses and chronic diseases.
• More than 40 healings of cancer.
• Cases involving "health upgrades."
• Cases involving healings of animals and even plants.
• A study of the connection between UFO abductions and psychic healing.
• Accounts in which people have been "rescued" by ETs.
• A study of miraculous cures from angels, NDEs, OBEs, lightning strikes, past life therapy, Native American ceremonial healings and more.
• Evidence that our governments have obtained UFO healing technology and are using it for themselves.
Who is being healed and why? What types of ETs are doing the healing? How are these healings being done? Are ETs our friends or foes? This massive 500-page book dives into the heart of the phenomenon and answers all these questions and more. Ignored for far too long, the UFO healing cases show a positive aspect to a phenomenon that has been saturated with disinformation for decades. The truth can no longer be denied. The aliens have arrived and as this book will show, one of their primary missions is the healing of all humanity.

Blue Giant Books
ISBN: 978-1984340702
226 pages

Undersea UFO Base

An In-Depth Investigation of USOs in the Santa Catalina Channel

For 100 years, strange activity has been occurring off the southern California Coast. Mile for mile, this area is one of the top producers of USOs (unidentified submersible objects) in the entire world. Drawing on firsthand testimonies from the Navy, Air Force, Coast Guard, police officers, lifeguards, residents and many others, Preston Dennett presents a compelling case for the possible existence of an undersea UFO base. Sightings of weird lights, anomalous glowing clouds, objects flying in and out of the water, mass UFO sightings, humanoid encounters--they're all here. More than ten years of research, presented here for the first time. The truth about this area can no longer be denied: something very strange is lurking in these waters.

- more than 70 cases of UFOs over the water.
- more than 70 cases of USOs in the water.
- original never before published cases.
- firsthand eyewitness testimonies from the Coast Guard, Navy and more.
- mass UFO sightings, some involving hundreds of objects.
- humanoid encounters, including abductions to an apparent base.
- An inside look at the History Channel's Deep Sea UFOs 1 & 2 & UFO Hunters.
- maps showing the location of all the activity.
- an in-depth exploration of the "Malibu Anomaly."
- photographs of UFOs and USOs, witnesses and encounter locations.
- original USO accounts from across the world.

Is there really an Undersea UFO Base off the southern California Coast? The evidence can be found inside this unique and groundbreaking book.

Blue Giant Books
ISBN: 9781539700029
175 Pages

Inside UFOs

While most UFO books are re-hashes of old cases, *"Inside UFOs"* presents the cutting edge of UFO research with ten all new original cases of extensive contact. A wide variety of ETs are presented, including various types of grays, Praying Mantis-type ETs, humanoids and Nordics. The witnesses are normal everyday people who suddenly find themselves in very unusual situations. The unique and unusual nature of the cases in this book will surprise even those well-versed in the UFO literature.

- A Navy Corpsman is invited aboard a UFO by his shipmate, only to meet fifteen-foot-tall friendly Praying Mantis-type ETs.
- A young child experiences an encounter with Nordic ETs that marks a lifelong series of contacts.
- A paperboy encounters a UFO and missing time, leaving him with an undiagnosed illness and a mystery that remained unsolved for years.
- An office-worker is confronted by a nine-foot-tall praying mantis, only to discover that she's also having contact with gray-type ETs too.
- a teacher stops on the road when a huge metallic sphere drops from the sky, and out steps a handsome-looking spaceman.
- A new mother is shocked to see an alien right outside her window, staring intently at her newborn son.
- a desperately ill housewife is transported from her home into an unknown base and cured by an eight-foot-tall orange-haired humanoid.
- A young farm-boy encounters UFOs on his family's farm, beginning a very close and lifelong relationship with ETs.
- A Navy Electronics Specialist has a complex UFO encounter aboard a Navy Ship, and is taught by the ETs about alternative energy sources.
- A nursing assistant has several missing time incidents culminating in a fully conscious encounter with gray ETs with an important message.

Why are the aliens here? What is their agenda on our planet? Are they hostile or benevolent? This book answers these questions and more, directly from the witnesses' themselves. This is not just another book about abductions by grays. This collection of true UFO stories shows how fascinating and bizarre ET contact can be.

Blue Giant Books
ISBN: 9780692650219
229 pages

Not from Here: Vol 1

The first of three volumes, this book reveals the stranger side to the UFO phenomenon. Drawing on cases from across the world, it shows just how bizarre the UFO phenomenon can be. A wide variety of topics are covered.

Conversations with Extraterrestrials. In most cases, ETs are very tight-lipped. But in some rare cases, people have held conversations with extraterrestrials.

Phone Call from an Alien. UFO contact is much stranger than most people can imagine. Contact occurs in many ways, sometimes even by telephone.

UFO--Don't Shoot. When faced with the unknown, it is human nature to shoot first and ask questions later. But what happens if you shoot at a UFO?

Alien Zoos. Are there zoos onboard UFOs? The answer is yes, and they contain many strange creatures, some from here and some not from here.

UFOs over Graveyards. Why are aliens hovering over graveyards? These spooky accounts are both surprising and unsettling.

They Walk Among Us. Sometimes aliens are seen in the strangest places, including bookstores, convenience stores, buses, train-stations, casinos, schools, subways and more.

The Alien-Clown Connection. Alien screen memories come in many forms, but the alien-clown connection is one of the strangest of all.

The Intimidation and Murder of UFO Witnesses. Many UFO witnesses have learned the hard way that it can be very dangerous to be a UFO witness.

Exposed--Project Redlight. Not all UFOs are being piloted by ETs. In some cases, the pilots appear to be the U.S. military. Are we flying the flying saucers?

Mining Data on UFOs. UFOs appear to have multiple agendas, including an active interest in mines and the precious metals of our planet.

Blue Giant Books
ISBN: 9781532804588
211 pages

Not from Here: Vol 2

The UFO phenomenon is profoundly strange and complex. This series of books focus on the strange and unusual cases, the kind that don't fit the standard model of UFO contact.

UFO Investigator's Disease. a collection of cases in which UFO researchers become themselves investigated by UFOs. It's a clear case of the hunter become the hunted.

Aliens-R-Us. In some cases in which ETs tell people that the reason they were contacted is because they and the ETs are related.

The Incredible Shrinking Abductee. Sometimes people are affected by ET technology in ways that are mindboggling, including being shrunken down in size.

The Mystery of Angel Hair. It's a strange web-like substance emitted from UFOs. Nobody knows what it is or what it means. In this huge collection of cases, some surprising answers are reyealed.

Extraterrestrial Gardeners. Aliens are conducting a comprehensive study of our planet. They are collecting samples of all kinds of plants, and affecting plants in bizarre ways.

UFO Rescue at Sea. It almost never happens, but in a few isolated cases, castaways lost at sea have been rescued by a UFO.

The Smell of UFOs. What do UFOs smell like? This is one of the largest collection of cases of UFO odors ever assembled. An analysis provides some surprising insights.

The UFO Breathing Pool. In one of the strangest of onboard experiences, abductees are placed inside a pool and made to breathe the liquid.

Alien Drinks. Sometimes people are given liquids by the ETs and told to drink them. The question is, why?

UFOs and Rockets. UFOs have been observed monitoring a wide variety of rocket and missile launches across the world. These cases show that ETs are keeping a very close eye on our explorations into deep space.

Blue Giant Books
ISBN: 9781719142748
183 pages

Not from Here: Vol 3

Diving deep into the heart of the UFO phenomenon, this volume (like the others) explores the weirder cases, the ones many UFO investigators don't like to talk about.

Caught in the Act. Although abductions number in the thousands or more, almost nobody ever sees an abduction happen. Or do they? The answer is yes, as these cases prove.

See a UFO--Lose Your Job. While seeing a UFO can be an exciting event, it sometimes comes with hidden dangers. Sometimes, seeing a UFO can even cost a person their job.

Alien Gifts. In very rare cases, aliens give people gifts, actual physical proof of their encounter. It almost never happens, but when it does, the results are astounding.

To Err is Alien. ETs are clearly more advanced than humans. But they are not perfect. Sometimes they make stupid mistakes.

Can We Contact UFOs with a Ouija Board? Usually used to communicate with spirits, there are now several cases in which the Ouija board is used to contact ETs.

UFOs over Prisons. UFOs are known to be attracted to nuclear power plants, military installations and other technological areas, including prisons. The question is, why?

Is Jesus an Alien? It's a question that's been asked many times, with few answers. There are now a number of cases in which people claim to have met Jesus aboard a UFO.

Is Bigfoot an Alien? Most UFO cases do not involve Bigfoot, and most Bigfoot cases do not involve UFOs. But in a tiny percentage of cases, these two phenomena perfectly intersect.

The Truth Behind Alien Anal Probes. Are people actually being anally probed by ETs? And if so, why? What exactly are the ETs looking for?

If You Build It. Abductees are often taken into the engine room of a UFO and told how it works. Some abductees have used their knowledge to actually build an alien engine.